FIGHTING FOR LOVE

THE SCIENCE OF HIGH-CONFLICT, PASSIONATE RELATIONSHIPS

RENAE C. LINDE

CRF Luttrell

Copyright © 2025 by Cynthia RF Luttrell

ISBN: 979-8-9990516-1-5

All rights reserved.

No portion of this book may be reproduced, stored, or transmitted in any form or by any means, electronic, mechanical, photocopying, recording, or otherwise, without the prior written permission from the copyright owner, except in the case of brief quotations embodied in reviews or articles as permitted by U.S. copyright law.

Independent Publication by CRF Luttrell

Contents

Introduction	1
PART I: The Foundations of Friction	5
1. Love, Conflict, and the Dance of Opposites	7
2. Attachment Styles – The Blueprint of Relationships	31
3. Engagement-Seeking Behavior – Why Some People Poke the Bear	53
PART II: Navigating the Highs and Lows	81
4. Control vs. Autonomy – The Fine Line Between Disengagement & Dismissal	83
5. The Power Struggle – Who Wins When No One Backs Down?	105

6. Breaking Points – The Moments That Define a Relationship — 125

PART III: Breaking Patterns, Building Strength — 147

7. Emotional Triggers and the Science of Reactivity — 149

8. The Recalibration Process – Finding the Right Balance — 177

9. Can You Change a Partner Who Thrives on Resistance? — 203

PART IV: The Resilient Marriage – Making It Work (Or Not) — 223

10. Love and War – When a Relationship Is Worth Fighting For — 225

11. The Art of Repair – What Happens After the Battle — 253

12. Unstoppable, Immovable, and Still Standing — 277

Conclusion: The Strength in Resistance — 299

References — 303

INTRODUCTION

When Immovable Meets Unstoppable

There's a story Jack likes to tell. A battleship captain notices a light ahead and radios a warning: "Unidentified vessel, change your course twenty degrees to starboard." The reply comes back: "Recommend you change your course." Irritated, the captain presses: "This is the captain of a U.S. Navy battleship. I say again, divert your course." The reply is simple, final: "This is a lighthouse. Your call."

We tell this story when we're trying to laugh through the fact that sometimes, in this relationship, no one moves.

One of us is the unstoppable force, dead set on impact. The other is the immovable object, grounded, bracing, absolutely refusing to shift. And what looks like disaster from the outside, two powers colliding, feels, from the inside, like the only honest kind of intimacy.

This book is about those relationships. The ones that are full of tension, full of fire, full of everything that makes other people say, "How do you live like that?" But we do live like that. Not in spite of the conflict, but through it.

In most relationships, conflict is a detour. In these, it's the main road.

And yet, not all conflict is connection. That's the hardest part. Somewhere in the wreckage of every fight, between the jabs and the silence and the moments that go too far, comes the question: Are we doing this because we love each other, or because we don't know how to stop?

Some couples can't stand the tension. Others can't stand the quiet. This book is for the latter, the ones who would rather fight than disappear, who feel more alive in the friction than they do in the calm. But that energy, that refusal to disengage, is a double-edged blade. It can cut through numbness, or cut each other open.

So what happens when staying present feels like survival... and so does leaving?

What happens when the argument is the intimacy?

What happens when a fight becomes the only place where nothing is hidden?

There is no easy answer. Some relationships implode. Some evolve. Some walk the tightrope forever, one misstep away from collapse, one small shift from breakthrough.

This book isn't just a story, it's a framework, built from the research of psychologists, attachment theorists, and trauma specialists who've spent their lives mapping the emotional terrain most couples never speak about. We draw from their work to offer perspective, to understand why passion sometimes looks like provocation, why safety can feel like suffocation, and why some couples feel most connected in conflict.

And maybe, if we're lucky, or stubborn enough to stay with the tension, we'll learn something along the way. Not just about each other, but about ourselves. About the difference between connection and control, about the lines we draw too late or not at all, and about how love survives in the spaces we swore would break it.

This is not a manual for peace. It's an exploration of what happens when peace was never the point.

It is a story of pain, persistence, passion, and the battle to tell the difference between love that resists collapse... and love that collapses because no one will yield.

So here we are.

You can change your course, or brace for impact.

Your call.

PART I: THE FOUNDATIONS OF FRICTION

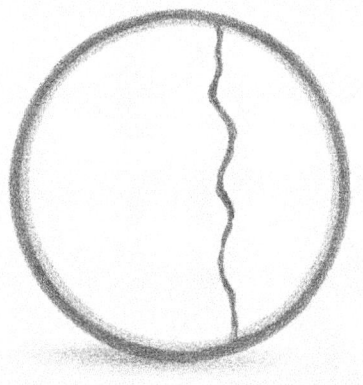

EXPLORE HOW CONFLICT BECOMES THE GLUE IN CERTAIN RELATIONSHIPS—WHY SOME COUPLES NEED THE TENSION TO FEEL ALIVE, AND WHERE THE LINE LIES BETWEEN CONNECTION AND COERCION.

Chapter One

Love, Conflict, and the Dance of Opposites

Why Some Couples Thrive on Tension

Love is often romanticized as a gentle force, something soothing, effortless, and free of struggle. But for some, love is a storm. It's a wild and unrelenting pull that demands attention, the force that keeps both partners locked in motion, each movement shaping the other. Some storms fortify. Others erode. And for couples like Jack and Lena, the line between the two was thin, so thin, they rarely noticed when they'd crossed it.

Lena never sought a relationship built on convenience. She was drawn to something else entirely, the kind of connection that demanded presence, challenged assumptions, and refused to be ignored. Jack was that force. From the moment they met, he was equal parts exhilarating and exasperating, pushing at the edges of her patience just as often as he pulled her in with undeniable charm. Their connection thrived on tension, the air between them always charged, like the sky before a thunderclap.

Jack had a way of coming at things sideways, never quite landing where she expected him to, and always forcing her to rethink her own footing. At first, it was exhilarating, they liked the same places, laughed at the same jokes, wanted the same kind of adventure. But there were moments when the way he looked at her felt like a setup, like he was testing for a reaction he'd already decided he wanted. She'd learned to keep up, to meet him where he wanted the conversation to go. But sometimes she had to wonder, was she engaging because she wanted to, or because not engaging felt like backing down?

He'd challenged her from the start, quick to ask why she thought the way she did. It wasn't condescending, not at first. It was curiosity, sharpened into provocation. The kind of energy that made her pulse quicken.

"You always have an answer for everything, don't you?" he'd teased one night after she picked apart his belief that doing the right thing is simple, you just do it.

"Yes, I do," she shot back smugly.

He laughed, and the way he looked at her then, like he'd found someone who wouldn't flinch at his fire, was what made it intoxicating. They weren't just talking; they were testing. Feeling for each other's edges. Seeing how much pressure the other could take before the shape shifted.

Love, stripped of its sentimental veneer, is often a negotiation of tensions. Real relationships aren't built on balance. They're built on contradiction. The need to be close and the need to protect space. The craving for stability and the ache for something wild. The longing for connection and the right to be unknown. These aren't flaws in love, they're its architecture.

Psychologists call this relational dialectics: the idea that human connection is shaped by opposing needs pulling at each other all the time (Baxter & Montgomery, 1996). For some couples, those tensions create friction. For others, they create momentum. Jack and Lena lived in the space between. Their relationship didn't "work" in the traditional sense. It pulsed, fluctuated, shifted. Sometimes they balanced. Sometimes they didn't. But they kept coming back to the tension, not to fix it, but to live inside it.

But when does that tension stop being connective and start eroding trust? When does resistance turn from play into control?

The tension between stability and change was the fuel in their dynamic. At least, that's how it used to feel.

Lately, Lena wasn't so sure. What once felt like electricity now felt like static, constant, invasive, impossible to shut out. She didn't pull back because she was tired. She pulled back because staying engaged meant losing too much of herself. She still craved the spark. But more and more, she caught herself flinching at the sound of his voice when it took on that edge, the one that meant he was winding up for another round. Another challenge. Another "conversation" that left her drained.

Some days, she wasn't sure if she was participating or just surviving.

While other couples sought comfort in predictability, Jack and Lena had always needed movement. Challenge. Uncertainty. But now Lena found herself wondering, was she still thriving in the chaos, or just bracing for it?

Their dynamic was becoming more about enduring contradictions rather than solving them. But lately, that endurance felt less like resilience and more like slow erosion.

For them, conflict had never been a threat, it was a language. A rhythm. Something that proved they were still reaching. While others tiptoed around disagreement, Jack and Lena leaned in. To them, friction didn't signal disconnection, it meant they were still in it.

But Jack didn't just lean in, he set the terms. When to push. When to engage. When to pull her back in if she dared to withdraw. For Lena, the rules weren't mutual. And lately, she was starting to see that.

She could roll her eyes. Scoff. Say she didn't want to talk about it. But they both knew better. This was how they stayed connected. Beneath the annoyance was a kind of pact, unspoken but binding, that neither would ever settle for passivity.

They felt it in their bodies, the electric charge of a sharp debate, the strange high that came from colliding without collapsing. Some couples sidestepped conflict to keep the peace. Jack and Lena used it to keep the signal alive.

Research suggests that for some couples, conflict can serve as a form of engagement rather than a symptom of division. High-energy interactions can stimulate emotional arousal and create an illusion of intimacy, especially in relationships where connection is tethered to emotional charge (Fisher, 2004; Tatkin, 2016). The key is in how conflict is managed, and whether both partners get to opt in.

For Jack and Lena, the tension wasn't about destruction. Not intentionally. It was about presence. They weren't trying to win. They were trying to stay in orbit.

The Myth of Perfect Harmony

We're taught that love should be easy. That if it's right, it won't be hard. That good relationships hum with harmony and mutual understanding. But real love, especially the kind that tries to hold tension without tipping into chaos, is far messier. What Jack and Lena wanted wasn't fire or stillness. It was a rhythm they could live with, steady enough to feel safe, sharp enough to keep them awake. And that kind of connection doesn't always come dressed as agreement.

Conflict isn't necessarily a sign of dysfunction. Often, it's a sign that both people are still invested. Still watching. Still reacting.

People assume happy couples fight less. But that's not true. The best couples don't avoid conflict, they just learn how to fight without leaving scars. Relationship researcher Dr. John Gottman has spent decades studying what makes love last, and what makes it rot from the inside out. His findings? It's not the frequency of conflict that determines longevity. It's how couples repair after damage is done (Gottman & Silver, 1999). Suppressing disagreement doesn't lead to connection. It leads to distance. And unspoken resentment has a way of becoming permanent.

For Jack, conflict wasn't about the fight. It was about knowing Lena hadn't slipped away. If she was arguing, she was still in it. And for Lena, there were times she let him believe he'd won a fight just so she could withdraw without drawing more heat. Their dynamic didn't run on harmony. It ran on tension. But for them, that wasn't failure. It was vitality. The struggle wasn't just a test, it was the proof that neither had given up.

They weren't dancing in perfect step. They were pushing, bracing, shifting, always trying to find where the edge was, without falling off it.

The Science of Constructive Conflict

Lena believed in peaceful relationships. She believed that if you could stay rational, if you could name what was happening instead of reacting to it, you wouldn't need blow-ups to get your point across. Jack didn't need a reason to spar. Sometimes he just needed the friction, the back-and-forth, the weight of someone pushing back.

And maybe, in their way, that was a kind of intimacy too.

The arguments, the debates, the constant back-and-forth, it wasn't just about proving a point. It was about proving they were still there. Still locked in. Still reaching for something neither of them could fully name.

Conflict isn't just about winning. It's about information. It reveals what matters. It shows where the fault lines are. The difference between guessing what your partner needs and hearing it, raw, unscripted, maybe even shouted, is the difference between performance and presence.

But not all conflict is created equal.

Destructive conflict erodes trust. It hijacks safety and replaces it with control. In those moments, the argument isn't about connection, it's about power. Constructive conflict, by contrast, is rooted in a shared desire to repair. It requires both partners to stay present, even when it's hard. Even when it hurts.

And for couples like Jack and Lena, that's the line they walked daily, sometimes blindfolded.

The Attraction of Opposition

It's no accident that some people are drawn to partners who challenge them. Psychologists studying relational dialectics have long argued that human connection doesn't form in perfect balance, it thrives in the tension between opposing needs: closeness and space, predictability and novelty, vulnerability and self-protection (Baxter & Montgomery, 1996). For some couples, these contradictions create friction. For others, they are the very fuel that keeps the relationship alive.

Dr. Helen Fisher, a biological anthropologist, has spent decades researching romantic attraction and partner selection. She found that people are often subconsciously drawn to traits that contrast their own. This isn't because opposites magically complete each other. Difference creates energy, something unfamiliar, unpredictable, alive (Fisher, 2004). The key isn't whether two people are similar. It's whether their differences lead to growth, or erode the bond over time.

Why We're Drawn to Tension

Not everyone fears conflict. For some, tension is how connection is felt. While many avoid relational friction to maintain calm, others move toward it, to spark engagement, to feel the current of being emotionally alive. It's not dysfunction. It's how some people know they matter.

Jack and Lena weren't drawn together despite their differences, they were drawn because of them. Where one pushed, the other pushed back. Where one tested, the other rose to meet it. Conflict, for them, wasn't a threat to the structure, it was confirmation it could hold. They didn't just withstand tension; they relied on it to prove they still fit together. When they clashed, it felt like a pulse check, something neither of them could fully explain, only feel.

But not every fight is about connection. Sometimes it's about control. About who gets to set the pace. About who decides when the engagement ends. Dr. Stan Tatkin (2012) argues that conflict can either be connective or corrosive. When driven by emotional engagement, it creates intimacy. When driven by power, it creates distance. Dr. Gottman's research echoes this, couples who challenge each other with curiosity rather than contempt report deeper emotional bonds and higher long-term satisfaction (Gottman & Silver, 1999).

In the beginning, Lena didn't question what their tension meant. The heat of their debates felt like sharp, little barbs. That meant she and Jack were still in it. Still participating. Still pushing. But lately, something was amiss. The teasing that once felt playful now carried an edge. The challenges that once energized her now made her brace.

The line between connection and coercion had blurred.

Conflict can strengthen a relationship, but only if both people have the freedom to step away. The most enduring oppositional couples are the ones who know how to read that moment. When to lean in, and when to back off. Jack and Lena were just starting to notice the difference. Maybe, deep down, they already knew, and the question was whether they'd admit it.

When Friction Becomes Fatigue

Tension can feed desire, but not endlessly. Over time, even the most engaging dynamics can begin to break down if conflict becomes the only form of contact.

Some of the early warning signs aren't explosive. They're subtle.

- Arguments that never resolve, just repeat in new costumes.
- Jokes that start to sting more than they soften.
- One partner leaving an exchange not more connected, but quietly exhausted.

Jack and Lena had always orbited intensity. But lately, Lena felt herself burning out. Arguments that once left her feeling closer now lingered in her body for hours. Her fuse was shortening. Her patience, fraying. The same tension that had once tethered them was starting to unravel her.

Research backs this trajectory. Chronic conflict doesn't just damage relationships, it rewires the people in them. Prolonged emotional strain increases cortisol, making it harder to regulate emotion in the heat of conflict (Sapolsky, 2004). Over time, the body learns to protect itself by disengaging, long before the relationship ends (Huston & Melz, 2004).

For couples like Jack and Lena, whose bond is built on emotional charge, this creates a dangerous paradox: the very thing that once signaled connection begins to threaten it.

How High-Tension Couples Stay Together

Oppositional dynamics can last, but not by accident. They survive on skill. Research by Dr. Terri Orbuch (2012) found that long-term, high-conflict couples who stayed emotionally connected shared three consistent habits:

1. Intentional De-escalation – They knew when to pause an argument before it became destructive.

2. Affection Amid Disagreement – They preserved warmth, even mid-conflict. A touch. A smile. A reminder that the argument wasn't the relationship.

3. Critique Boundaries – They challenged each other's ideas, not each other's worth.

Jack and Lena had no script for this. No language for what was shifting. What once felt like shared spark was now drifting toward imbalance. And neither knew how to name it without tearing the whole thing down.

Reconnecting Without Rupture

Tension didn't ruin Jack and Lena. In many ways, it defined them. But what made their relationship endure wasn't the conflict, it was what happened after. The laughter that returned unprompted. The sideways glance after a fight. The way they always circled back to each other, even when they didn't have the words.

Still, there's a line. And Tatkin warns it's easy to cross. When challenge becomes criticism, when intensity becomes chronic, when every disagreement leaves behind scar tissue, that's no longer engagement. That's erosion.

Oppositional couples can thrive. But they can't survive on friction alone.

Sustaining the connection requires other anchors, ones that don't spark, but settle.

- Shared humor that diffuses the heat.
- Collaborative focus, projects or routines that don't revolve around conflict.
- Physical closeness that reconnects them without a single word.

These moments, small and quiet, are what keep high-conflict relationships from becoming high-cost ones.

Regulating the Fire

The key difference between couples who survive tension and those who burn out isn't how often they fight. It's how well they regulate themselves in the process.

Neuroscience research shows that couples who manage conflict constructively activate the brain's regulatory systems, particularly the prefrontal cortex, which governs impulse control and decision-making (Davidson & Begley, 2012). It's not about suppressing emotion. It's about creating space between trigger and reaction.

Emotional regulation means:
- Noticing when your pulse is climbing.
- Pausing before you throw your sharpest words.
- Shifting perspective before the conversation hardens into battle.

Jack and Lena didn't talk about emotional regulation. They wouldn't have called it that anyway. In the beginning, it just looked like instinct, pausing before things went too far, trading sarcasm for softness when one of them edged too close to a nerve. The stakes weren't high yet. They didn't know each other's buttons, only that there were some, and getting close to them felt like part of the fun.

They were oppositional, but not reckless. Their friction didn't feel like a threat, it felt like chemistry. But even then, the pattern was forming. Not just the fight, but the return. The pull back in. The quiet decision to stay close, even after the spark left a mark.

The Nature of Conflict Over Time

Conflict isn't something most couples plan for, it evolves. In the early stages of a relationship, disagreements feel like tests. Where are the lines? What does the other person really mean when they say, "I'm fine"? But over time, patterns emerge. Not just in how couples argue, but in how they repair. Whether conflict becomes a wedge or a tether often depends less on what's said and more on how both people show up when the dust settles.

Relationship researcher Dr. Terri Orbuch found that the way couples handle conflict in the first five years of marriage is one of the strongest predictors of long-term satisfaction. The difference lies in orientation, those who treat disagreements as opportunities to solve problems rather than personal attacks are the ones who tend to last (Orbuch, 2012).

Jack and Lena's dynamic followed a similar arc. In the beginning, their conflicts flared quick, playful one minute, defensive the next, more reflex than strategy. But over time, a rhythm emerged. They learned each other's triggers. Jack sensed when Lena was distancing, but he didn't always take the hint. Lena learned that Jack didn't just bristle at criticism, he braced for it. Their arguments didn't vanish, but they shifted. What once felt like chaos started to feel practiced, almost instinctual.

There's a biological reason for that. Repeated exposure to conflict, when it doesn't escalate into trauma, can actually improve emotional regulation. The brain learns to tolerate discomfort, strengthening the neural pathways that make resolution possible (Panksepp, 1998).

But not all learning comes easy. Personal history writes its own scripts.

Lena had been raised to keep her thoughts tight, her reactions tighter. Disagreement in her home wasn't safe, it was something to survive. So when Jack challenged her, it didn't always feel engaging. Sometimes, it felt like pressure. And eventually, like a threat. Jack, on the other hand, was wired differently. Debate, in his world, meant relevance. If he was arguing with you, he was still in it. Silence, to him, felt like he didn't exist.

Their early conflicts weren't just about the present. They were reenactments. His insistence. Her withdrawal. His escalation. Her exit. Their fights weren't about winning. They were about survival, but they hadn't realized that yet.

Many couples interpret the shift from emotionally charged arguments to more measured disagreements as emotional decline. But in reality, this transition often marks growth, a movement from impulsive reactivity to intentional connection. The goal isn't fewer conflicts. It's fewer unrepairable ones.

The Psychological and Biological Effects of Conflict

Constructive conflict doesn't just help a relationship. It rewires the brain. When couples feel heard, the prefrontal cortex, the region responsible for rational thought and self-control, stays engaged. But when arguments spiral, the brain flips into survival mode. Cortisol floods the body, impulse control tanks, and the chance for resolution disappears (Sapolsky, 2004).

Jack and Lena's relationship held both of these possibilities. Their early debates sparked something alive. It made them sharp, focused, hungry to understand each other. But that energy had a cost. Tension left unchecked started to linger. What once pulled Lena in began to wear her down.

When conflict becomes chronic, the body treats the relationship as a threat. Over time, couples lose the ability to co-regulate. They stop listening. They brace. They wait for the next blow. Emotional safety erodes, replaced by vigilance (Mikulincer & Shaver, 2007). You stop hearing your partner and start hearing your past. In that space, even a small disagreement can feel like a breach.

The Science of Push-Pull Attraction

For some people, emotional opposition creates a sense of closeness, not because they enjoy chaos, but because the uncertainty keeps them present. Neuroscience supports this. The brain responds to unpredictable emotional patterns the same way it responds to high-stakes gambling, anticipation creates a dopamine surge, reinforcing the sense of emotional investment (Fisher, 2004).

For couples with insecure attachment, particularly those who are fearful-avoidant, conflict becomes both threat and proof of connection. It's not about harmony. It's about the emotional current that says, "We're still in it." That push-pull becomes addictive. It keeps partners emotionally alert, constantly reaching, never resting.

Jack and Lena thrived in this space. Friction wasn't just tolerated, it was interpreted as intimacy. They tested each other not to destroy, but to confirm. Are you still here? Are you still choosing me?

This interplay between closeness and resistance can create remarkable emotional resilience, if the foundation includes mutual respect and emotional safety. But that's the line many couples don't realize they're crossing until it's too late.

Healthy friction heightens engagement. Destructive conflict erodes it. The difference lies in whether both people can walk away from an argument still believing they're on the same team.

When Connection Turns to Volatility

Friction only builds intimacy when buffered by security. Without that safety net, even small tensions become loaded. Studies in affective neuroscience and attachment theory show that couples need to trust that disagreement won't unravel the relationship (Coan et al., 2006). Otherwise, conflict turns from connection into volatility, amplifying doubt instead of reinforcing closeness.

It's a subtle shift, but once it begins, the damage compounds.

Lena felt it in her body before she could name it. That split-second hesitation before responding. The careful calibration of tone. The way she stayed alert during conversations that used to feel playful. Jack still needed the resistance, but she was starting to feel the cost of supplying it.

This is the line oppositional couples walk, the one between engagement and erosion. When conflict is grounded in security, it strengthens the bond. When it becomes a substitute for emotional access, it wears the connection thin.

How Culture Shapes Relationship Conflict

The way couples experience conflict isn't just shaped by personality. It's shaped by context, family systems, cultural norms, and the stories we grow up believing about what love is supposed to look like. Some cultures prize harmony. Others value direct engagement. Studies on intercultural communication show that cultural background heavily influences whether conflict is viewed as a threat to connection or a sign of investment (Ting-Toomey, 2005).

Lena had never been afraid of conflict, not in theory. She'd grown up in a house where discipline came swift and rules weren't up for discussion. But she learned early that power didn't belong to the loudest voice, it belonged to the one who refused to be moved. Her father didn't raise his voice because he was never in the fight to begin with. He stayed quiet, distant, as if the household didn't concern him. Her mother made up for it, loud, certain, and immovable. Every conversation was a verdict. There was no reasoning with that kind of certainty. So Lena stopped trying.

Lena wasn't raised to yell her way through an argument. Yelling didn't get you anywhere, not with someone who always had the last word, and not with someone who never said anything at all. She learned to hold the line. If you didn't react, they couldn't twist your words. If you didn't engage, they couldn't pull you in. But not every fight plays by those rules. Some people don't back down unless they're met with equal force. And Lena had learned, sometimes, the only way to stay standing was to meet fire with fire.

Then came Jack.

Jack didn't just challenge her. He set the tempo. He didn't want silent resistance or implied boundaries, he wanted the fire, the engagement, the full-force response. But always on his timeline. Always on his terms. At first, it felt electric. Lena finally felt like she wasn't the only one who believed that tension could be connective. That a relationship built on challenge could also be deeply alive. But over time, she started to wonder: was she showing up because she wanted to, or because, with Jack, pulling back never felt like a real option?

Their dynamic mirrored what psychologists describe as a Western engagement model, where direct conflict signals honesty, and silence is interpreted as withdrawal. But neither of them came to that style clean.

Lena hadn't been raised to believe peace came easily. She learned that peace came through control, through saying less, reacting less, needing less. It was something you protected, not something you expected. But with Jack, peace wasn't the baseline. Conflict wasn't just tolerated, it was embedded in the way they loved. Disagreements weren't ignored, but they weren't always resolved either. Some were just absorbed. Others were carried quietly for later.

Jack hadn't grown up in a house where conflict meant connection. His father enforced order. His mother tried to soften the edges. But with eight brothers and sisters spread across years and tempers, the real battles were horizontal, between siblings, especially the older ones. Jack learned early that survival wasn't about being the loudest, it was about knowing when to push back and when to disappear. He didn't avoid conflict. He came up in it. Fought his brothers, out-dared his friends, tested boundaries just to see who'd blink first. Later, that instinct followed him. Conflict wasn't just noise. It was positioning. It was proof you hadn't lost your ground. To Jack, a partner who stopped pushing back was a partner who had already started to leave.

To outsiders, their relationship might have looked combative. But inside, it felt like oxygen. Neither of them feared engagement. They feared irrelevance.

Of course, it wasn't just culture. It was gender. It was era. Research shows that men and women are often conditioned to handle conflict differently. Women, more often than not, are socialized to prioritize emotional harmony. Men are more likely to externalize their distress through assertiveness, or withdrawal (Wood, 2013). But this wasn't just about roles. It was about what they absorbed in the quiet. Jack learned to assert or disengage. Lena learned to smooth things over or disappear. Neither of them learned what mutual conflict resolution looked like.

And so, their instincts collided.

What one couple sees as volatility, another interprets as vitality. The question isn't whether conflict is present. It's whether both partners agree on what purpose it serves.

How Other Couples Navigate High-Engagement Relationships

Jack and Lena weren't outliers. Plenty of couples operate with high emotional frequency, engaging often, pushing each other, challenging ideas, drawing boundaries and then testing them. A study by Huston and Melz (2004) found that couples with moderate-to-high conflict early in their relationships were often more resilient long-term than those who prioritized politeness over engagement.

In a decade-long study, researchers observed married couples and found that those who debated frequently, but respectfully, reported higher satisfaction than those who rarely engaged in open disagreement (Markman et al., 2010). The difference wasn't how much they fought. It was what the fights meant.

Emily and David were one of those couples. Married over fifteen years, their relationship was built on push and pull. Emily, an attorney, approached arguments like cases to be won. David, a philosophy professor, loved forcing her to defend her logic. Their disagreements were sharp, sometimes theatrical, but never cruel.

"It's how we connect," David once said. "If we stop challenging each other, we start fading."

What kept them close wasn't agreement. It was presence. For them, as for Jack and Lena, conflict wasn't chaos. It was commitment in another language.

The Importance of Mutual Respect

Dr. Alexandra Solomon (2017) describes couples like these as "high-intensity connectors." They argue. They push. They get loud. But they also know how to return to center. The

distinction between connection and volatility lies in what happens afterward.
- Do both partners feel heard and understood?
- Can they reset the emotional temperature without holding onto resentment?
- Do their fights challenge ideas, or attack character?

Jack and Lena didn't always know where the line was, but they could feel when they were getting close. Their bond wasn't built on peace, it was built on the pull. The instinct to come back, even when nothing was resolved. Sometimes it looked like sarcasm. Sometimes like brushing shoulders in a doorway. Sometimes just not leaving, even when they both wanted to.

Not all high-engagement couples get it right.

The difference between engagement and erosion is subtle. It's when criticism replaces curiosity. When the argument stops being about understanding and starts being about punishment. Dr. Stan Tatkin identifies two critical ingredients that separate healthy tension from destructive cycles: emotional safety and repair. If either is missing, the conflict starts to rot the foundation instead of reinforcing it (Tatkin, 2012).

How Memory Shapes the Emotional Impact of Conflict

What couples carry forward from conflict isn't just the facts, it's the story they tell themselves about what it meant. Research on relational memory suggests that how couples recall past tension shapes how they approach future disagreements (Holmes & Rempel, 2012).

When memories of conflict are layered with resolution, laughter, or mutual understanding, even heated moments can become part of the couple's shared emotional scaffolding. But when the emotional residue of past fights lingers, new disagreements arrive already charged. Partners start fighting with ghosts.

Jack and Lena didn't know it at the time, but they stored their unresolved arguments like ammo. They hadn't learned to reframe conflict yet. Sometimes they joked about it. Sometimes they just moved on like nothing happened. But nothing ever fully left the room.

Negativity bias in memory causes couples to fixate on unresolved pain, making each new conflict feel like the beginning of the end. In contrast, positive conflict recall, the ability to look back on past tension and see growth instead of failure, reinforces resilience. (Rozin & Royzman, 2001).

That kind of memory isn't accidental. It's adaptive.

Jack and Lena's connection wasn't there yet. It was built on what they held onto, and what they refused to let go of. But the risk was starting to surface. The fire that kept them connected was the same fire that could consume them.

Still, neither of them wanted to test how far that line could bend before it finally broke.

Next: Attachment Styles – The Blueprint of Relationships

Before we can fully understand why some couples fight like it's survival, and love like it's the same thing, we have to trace the roots. Not just of how they argue, but how they engage. How they come close. How they pull away. How they stay, even when staying feels combustible.

Attachment theory gives us that map.

Originally developed by John Bowlby (1969) and expanded by Mary Ainsworth (1978), attachment theory explores the deep-seated patterns that form early in life and follow us into adulthood, shaping how we bond, how we cope, and how we protect ourselves from emotional threat.

Attachment isn't just about neediness or distance. It's about nervous systems. Memory. Muscle. It's the language we speak when we're scared, even when we don't know we're scared. It shows up in how we fight, how we apologize, and how we reach for each other after the tension breaks.

Some people seek security in predictability. Others find it in motion, in the testing, in the tension, in the constant confirmation that the other person is still there, still pushing back.

Jack and Lena are the latter.

Their dynamic isn't about one person chasing and the other running. It's about two people trying to stay close while protecting the parts of themselves that have never felt entirely safe. Their fights aren't just about the present, they're echoes of the past, rehearsals for survival. And the reason it feels like fire isn't because it's doomed. It's because, for some, heat is how love is proven.

In Chapter 2, we'll dig into the attachment styles that shape this kind of relationship, the ones that make friction feel familiar, even necessary. We'll explore how the avoidant instinct to flee and the anxious instinct to pursue can coexist in the same person. And how, in couples like Jack and Lena, these patterns don't just clash, they cycle. They reverse. They repeat.

Understanding attachment is the first step to understanding the relationships that don't fit the mold, and the people who fight, not because they're trying to leave, but because they're terrified of disappearing.

Chapter Two

Attachment Styles – The Blueprint of Relationships

Overview of Attachment Styles

The Evolution of Attachment Theory

Love is often spoken of as a mystery, an unexplainable force that draws people together in ways that defy logic. But in reality, our ability to love, and the way we go about it, isn't random at all. It follows a pattern, one that starts long before our first romance and shapes every relationship that follows.

Love isn't a mystery. It's a pattern.

Some people learn that love is safety, something steady they can trust. Others learn that love is a battlefield, something to earn, something that can be taken away. And once those lessons are learned, they don't disappear. They shape every fight, every silence, every impossible push and pull that comes after.

Jack and Lena didn't invent their dynamic. They inherited it.

Jack believed in self-sufficiency. You either handled your own problems, or you didn't. The past wasn't some ghost following him around, at least, that's what he told himself. Until Lena. Until their fights. Until the way her silence could gut him. The way she could disappear with a single look.

It was supposed to be different with her. And yet every sharp word, every retreat, every tense standoff between them felt familiar. Like he had played this game before, memorized the rules, and still didn't know how to win.

Psychologists like Bowlby had a name for this: attachment theory. Jack didn't care much for theories, but even he couldn't deny that patterns had a way of repeating. He pushed; Lena pulled back. He demanded engagement; she maintained distance. They weren't just fighting about dishes or tone of voice. They were reenacting lessons learned long before they met, lessons about what love was supposed to feel like, and whether safety was something earned or something freely given.

Jack and Lena weren't opposites. They were the same style of attachment, fractured into opposite directions. Both fearful-avoidant. Both shaped by trauma. Both operating from nervous systems that expected danger, even in love.

But Jack's fear showed up in volume, escalation, pressure, intensity. Lena's showed up in stillness, distance, retreat, withdrawal. He needed connection on his terms. She needed control over hers.

Their arguments weren't about winning. They were about not disappearing.

Every fight followed the same choreography, Jack advanced, Lena withdrew. He pushed, she paused. It was never just about the topic. It was about proving something neither could say aloud: that love had never been about peace. It had always been about resistance.

Jack didn't need a psychologist to tell him that the way people love, the way they fight, the way they hold on or pull away, is patterned. He knew it. He'd seen it. Not just in Lena, but in himself.

Some people sought safety in closeness. Some in distance. And some, like Jack and Lena, didn't know what they needed, only that stillness felt like danger, and chaos sometimes felt like proof that someone was still there.

Lena wasn't afraid of silence. She relied on it. She had learned early that space meant control, that distance kept her from being swallowed by someone else's emotions.

Jack couldn't tolerate silence. He needed a reaction, something to confirm she was still in it. If she pulled away, he pushed harder. If she shut down, he raised the stakes. He wasn't trying to fight, he was trying to keep her present.

The labels didn't matter much in the moment, anxious, avoidant, fearful-avoidant. What mattered was the pattern.

Jack pressed; Lena retreated. Lena withdrew; Jack chased. He didn't mean to push her to the edge, but silence hit him like a threat, not a puzzle to solve, but a presence to overpower. He escalated because force was the only language his nervous system trusted when connection felt at risk.

Why Conflict Feels Like Survival

What if the fight isn't about being right at all? Some are about staying visible. Some are about holding on. And some are about reclaiming control when everything else feels uncertain.

Jack and Lena's arguments weren't about dishes or tone. They were about survival. They were about preserving a sense of emotional gravity, proof that neither had vanished.

People like Jack, those whose early experiences made love feel unpredictable, don't just argue to make a point. They argue to prove they still matter. To be invisible was worse than being disliked. A fight, at least, confirmed presence.

Lena wasn't so different. Her retreat wasn't indifference, it was defense. She didn't escalate like Jack did, but every shutdown, every pause, every stillness was a strategy. Engaging on someone else's terms never ended well. She had learned that controlling her level of engagement was her only safety.

So when Jack pushed, she didn't meet him. It's not that she didn't care. She cared more about potentially losing herself in the process.

They weren't fighting about dinner plans or whether someone forgot to text. They were fighting to preserve themselves. To protect their individual emotional operating systems from collapse.

And sometimes, the roles reversed.

Sometimes it was Lena who confronted, Lena who pushed. And Jack who went quiet. Jack who shut down. When the tension built too far, or when Lena's questions cut too close, he backed off. This was his way of escaping the feeling that he was no longer in control of the narrative. Lena's pursuit wasn't neediness. It was urgency. She wanted answers. She wanted repair. But when she became the one chasing clarity, Jack became the one pulling away.

This was the hidden truth of fearful-avoidant attachment. The roles weren't fixed. They shifted based on perceived threat. When Jack felt threatened, he escalated to stay in control. When Lena felt threatened, she disengaged to protect herself. But over time, under chronic stress, their roles could, and did, flip. Lena began pursuing answers. Jack began dodging them.

It wasn't about who they were in essence. It was about which part of them was running the show.

The Anatomy of Escalation

Jack wasn't trying to start a fight. He just needed Lena to say something, anything.

She stood in the kitchen, arms crossed, face unreadable. Too unreadable. That's what got to him the most.

"Are you even listening to me?" His voice came out sharper than he intended.

"I heard you," she said, reaching for a glass. No irritation. No warmth. Just distance.

Jack felt his chest tighten. He knew this part. The moment where her silence said more than her words. The part where, no matter what he said next, she would drift into that unreachable place he couldn't follow.

It was just an argument. He knew that. But his body didn't. His nervous system was already primed, tight jaw, clenched hands, a deep sense of absence settling in his chest. He could feel himself tipping. That awful, familiar sensation of being shut out. Of becoming invisible.

Jack didn't trust stability. Lena didn't trust closeness. She avoided being cornered; he avoided being ignored.

It wasn't about theory, not in the moment, not when they were locked in that room with the tension rising and no one willing to back down. But the pattern was there, whether they wanted to see it or not.

Jack was fearful-avoidant, caught in the no-man's land between craving closeness and fearing what it might cost him. When he sensed distance, he didn't shut down. He engaged. Intensely. He didn't fade, he advanced. Even if that meant provoking a reaction just to avoid the silence.

Lena was fearful-avoidant too, but her survival instinct was different. She didn't test people to keep them close. She withheld to keep herself intact. Closeness had once meant compliance. Now, it meant risk. Her power came from managing what she let others access, and what she didn't.

And that's where the friction lived. Jack needed proof of connection. Lena needed control over when and how she engaged. He pushed. She withdrew. He demanded a response. She gave only what she was willing to lose.

This wasn't immaturity. It wasn't drama. It was a trauma pattern, one that neither of them had signed up for, but both of them recognized by feel alone.

It wasn't random. It was repetition.

The Power of the Quiet Aftermath

Conflict didn't rattle Jack. What unsettled him was what came after, silence, distance, disconnection. He could handle Lena's sharp words, even her sarcasm. What he couldn't handle was the hollow quiet that followed. The moments where she shut him out so completely it was as if he no longer existed.

And Lena? Silence had always been her power play. Words could be twisted. Emotions could be used against her. But withdrawal? That was one game no one could force her to play on their terms.

When Jack escalated, she shut down. When he pressed, she retreated. Not because she didn't care, but because caring without safety was not an option.

They weren't two people trying to find common ground. They were two people trying to survive each other.

Jack needed engagement to feel real. Lena needed distance to stay intact.

Every argument wasn't just about the surface issue. It was the same fight, over and over. It wasn't that they didn't learn. Learning wasn't the problem. Pattern was.

Recognition doesn't undo a trauma response. Jack and Lena weren't learning new ways to fight, they were perfecting the old ones.

Why This Matters for High-Conflict Relationships

Different attachment styles respond to conflict in different ways. Some de-escalate, soothe, seek resolution. Others brace, defend, escalate, not to harm, but to avoid being emotionally erased.

That's the trap for many high-conflict relationships. Conflict becomes proof of emotional presence. Silence becomes the real threat. And attachment theory becomes the missing piece, not to label behavior, but to trace it. To understand that what looks like volatility may actually be someone's way of staying emotionally tethered.

Jack and Lena weren't two opposites magnetically drawn to each other. They were both wired to want closeness, but terrified by the vulnerability it required. Their push-pull wasn't personality difference. It was survival instinct.

Jack sought closeness through control. Lena preserved autonomy through distance. Their styles weren't at odds, they were mirrors, fractured down the middle, reflecting different sides of the same unresolved fear.

Understanding attachment isn't a cure. But it is a compass. It helps high-conflict couples name the cycle, trace its roots, and, if they're willing, begin to navigate a different way forward.

Understanding where you've been is the first step toward changing where you're going.

How Early Experiences Shape Conflict Patterns in Adult Relationships

It starts before we ever say "I love you." Before our first heartbreak, our first argument, our first moment of wondering why relationships feel so complicated. The way we handle love, attachment, and, most importantly, conflict doesn't begin in adulthood. It's written into us long before we even know what a relationship is.

Our earliest experiences, the way our parents handled stress, how our caregivers responded to our emotions, the background static of unresolved tension, these become the blueprint. They dictate how we argue, when we withdraw, and whether conflict feels like a conversation, a threat, or a trap.

The Family Blueprint: What We Learn Before We Know We're Learning

Every family has its own native language of conflict. Some homes operate in cold war silence, tight air, no voices. Others are battlegrounds, raised tones, slammed doors, someone always winning and someone always losing. A few are diplomatic zones, where feelings are acknowledged, and problems are resolved without anyone having to raise their voice.

Children internalize these patterns long before they have the vocabulary to describe them. They learn what conflict means, emotionally, relationally, even if no one ever explains it out loud.

If they grew up with dismissiveness, they may associate emotional expression with rejection.

If they witnessed volatility, they may become explosive, or shut down entirely to survive.

If caregivers were inconsistent, they may link conflict to abandonment, constantly gauging whether love will hold or disappear.

This is why two people can have radically different reactions to the same argument. One sees conflict as productive; the other sees it as proof that something is breaking. The fight itself is irrelevant, the conflict is really about the emotional script that's being replayed beneath it.

A Tale of Two Arguments: How Early Experiences Shape Reactions

Let's take two people, Emma and Jake. They've been together for a few years, and like any couple, they argue from time to time. But it's not the content of their arguments that defines them, it's the choreography of their emotional responses.

Emma's Background: *The Peacemaker*

Emma grew up in a household where conflict was treated like a contaminant. Her parents rarely argued openly, and when they did, it was handled behind closed doors, with forced smiles at dinner. The message was clear: peace mattered more than truth, and discomfort was to be neutralized, not named.

Now, as an adult, Emma avoids conflict instinctively. She minimizes her needs, apologizes quickly, and sidesteps tension before it builds. Confrontation doesn't feel like communication, it feels like danger. Her nervous system is wired to equate intensity with instability. So when emotions rise, she folds. Not because she lacks opinions, but because voicing them never felt safe.

Jake's Background: *The Fighter*

Jake's house was the opposite. His parents argued loud and often, but always came back together. To him, raised voices weren't red flags, they were signs of life. Arguments meant people cared. Silence meant disconnection. If you didn't fight for it, it wasn't real.

So when Jake and Emma fight, he leans in. He wants to work through it, now, fully, loudly if needed. He believes resolution lives on the other side of confrontation. But Emma only hears a storm. The more he pushes, the more she disappears. The more she disappears, the harder he pushes.

They aren't trying to hurt each other. They're just reenacting the only emotional choreography they've ever known.

The Echo of Past Relationships: When Old Wounds Resurface

Families aren't the only social structure that teach us how to fight. Former partners do, too. Every argument leaves an imprint. Every betrayal rewrites the nervous system.

Someone who's been punished for honesty may grow quiet in future conflicts.

Someone gaslit into doubting their own reality may interrogate their partner's every word.

Someone who was only shown affection after apologizing may learn to collapse just to restore peace.

This is why seemingly small arguments can spiral so quickly. A short reply, a sigh, a delayed text, none of it is neutral when old wounds are still in the room. Conflict activates the current tension, and also the cumulative weight of past pain.

Jack and Lena lived this. Their fights weren't just about each other. They were layered, past relationships, childhood scripts, trauma responses flaring like alarms. At times, they were reacting less to the present moment and more to the ghosts it summoned.

There were nights Lena would confront Jack because she longed for truth. He'd withdraw, because her questions touched something raw. Then there were days when Jack would escalate, raise his voice, demand a response, because the silence felt like he'd been erased.

Their wounds were different, but they spoke the same language. Just with different accents.

How Trauma Responses Masquerade as Personality

Conflict isn't just about what's said. It's about what's felt, and what gets triggered beneath the surface. The words are rarely the whole story. The real tension lives in what the nervous system perceives as threat.

Some people feel overwhelmed in conflict. Their heart races, thoughts spin, voices sound louder than they are. They're certainly able to handle a little tension, but they panic because sometimes conflict registers as a threat to safety.

Others freeze. Shut down. Disengage. Not because they don't care, but because their body learned long ago that pulling away was the only way to feel safe.

These reactions don't come from logic. They come from conditioning. From what it once took to survive.

Studies in interpersonal psychology show that insecure attachment is closely linked to heightened physiological stress during conflict. When emotional safety is at risk, the body flips into fight, flight, or freeze mode (Pietromonaco & Powers, 2015). Arguments that seem minor from the outside can feel existential on the inside.

For the anxiously attached, conflict feels like abandonment in motion.

For the avoidantly attached, it feels like losing control.

And for the fearful-avoidant, the category Jack and Lena both occupy, it feels like both.

Fearful-avoidants live in contradiction. They crave closeness but distrust it. They seek connection but expect rejection. When conflict surfaces, they may chase one moment and retreat the next. Their emotional reflexes don't match their intent, which makes them feel unpredictable, even to themselves.

Jack and Lena: Two Sides of the Same Fear

Jack and Lena both had the same attachment style, but their trauma responses ran in opposite directions.

Jack chased connection through escalation. If Lena grew quiet, he raised his voice. If she disengaged, he pushed harder. He didn't want control for its own sake, he wanted to feel anchored. Conflict was his way of tethering her. If she fought back, she was still with him. If she didn't, he feared she was already gone.

Lena, by contrast, preserved her sense of control through distance. When Jack pushed, she pulled back. When he pressed harder, she disappeared further. But not out of spite. Out of survival. If she couldn't control the emotional pace, she couldn't trust the space. And if she couldn't trust the space, she shut it down.

But under enough stress, especially prolonged or emotionally destabilizing stress, their roles flipped.

Lena, who once resisted pursuit, began to seek clarity. Not with pleading, but with pressure. She wanted answers, accountability, repair. And Jack, who once demanded connection, began to retreat. He felt ambushed by her need for resolution. His internal logic flipped: pursuing felt vulnerable. Dodging felt safer.

This is where most advice about "pursuers and withdrawers" misses the mark. Jack and Lena weren't static roles. Their reactions were fluid, driven by fear, trauma, and emotional exposure. Their shared attachment style meant both feared engulfment and abandonment, just in different ways, at different times.

When Conflict Isn't About the Present

By the time an argument erupted between Jack and Lena, the thing they were actually arguing about was rarely the cause. A look, a pause, a misread tone, those were just the triggers. The actual conflict was older. Deeper. The real fight was about fear, of disconnection, of loss, of being misunderstood or overpowered.

They weren't fighting about each other. Not really. They were fighting with everything that came before each other.

That's what makes attachment-driven conflict so disorienting. It feels personal, but it isn't. It's not about who left the cabinet open or the wording of a text. It's about what that silence meant in childhood, or the body remembering what it meant to be dismissed.

If partners don't understand the roots of these reactions, they'll think they're incompatible. In reality, they may just be in survival mode, each reenacting a pattern that once kept them safe.

Recognizing this doesn't excuse bad behavior. It helps us understand what drives it. Because the moment you can name a pattern, you can stop being ruled by it.

The Jack & Lena Dynamic: A Push-Pull Between Independence and Reassurance

Jack and Lena weren't doomed from the start, but their relationship wasn't built on ease. It was built on friction. They loved each other, certainly, but theirs was a fundamental mismatch in how they each pursued emotional safety.

Jack, fearful-avoidant with control-driven volatility, didn't view conflict as a threat. He saw it as a tool, something that kept him emotionally tethered to Lena. Whether it came through teasing, debate, or outright provocation, his engagement wasn't random. If she was reacting, she was present. If she was quiet, disengaged, neutral, that's when the alarm bells rang. He didn't want to dominate her. He just didn't want to disappear.

Lena, also fearful-avoidant, coped through self-protection. Where Jack escalated, she maintained distance. Where he pushed to keep the connection alive, she stepped back to keep from being swallowed. Her silence wasn't passive-aggression. It was defense. She'd learned early that emotional intensity came at a cost, and that cost was usually her.

This was the loop: Jack pursued to feel connected. Lena disengaged to stay intact.

Why They Were Drawn to Each Other

People don't just fall into relationships by accident. They gravitate toward what feels familiar. Not necessarily what feels good, what feels known.

Jack and Lena weren't opposites. They were the same attachment style, split down the middle by trauma. Two fearful-avoidants reacting to the same core fear, of being too much, not enough, or left behind, just in opposing ways.

Jack had grown up equating control with safety. Vulnerability wasn't an option, it was an opening to be hurt. So he learned to stay emotionally active by staying emotionally dominant. If he could steer the conversation, push the tempo, provoke the response, he could keep the ground under his feet.

Lena learned to manage emotional energy like currency. She could read people before they spoke. Knew how to respond, how to retreat, when to feign calm. Her survival wasn't in taking control, it was in refusing to be controlled.

So when Jack challenged her, she didn't retreat immediately. She met him. Matched him. Not because she wanted to spar, but because she knew how to hold a line. He thrived on that. It proved she wasn't passive. It proved she cared.

If Lena had ignored him from the beginning, Jack might have let her go. But she didn't. She met him halfway, just long enough to spark something real, and just far enough back to keep it unstable.

The Emotional Tug-of-War

Jack didn't think he was starting fights. He was just being himself, saying what came to mind, probing for engagement, pressing when he felt her pull away. If Lena went quiet, he raised the stakes. He wasn't trying to create conflict. He was trying to make sure she hadn't disappeared.

But when Lena reacted, whether she pushed back, shut down, or turned away, he saw her as the one turning it into a fight. In his mind, he was just keeping the conversation alive.

It never occurred to him that what felt like connection to him might feel like intrusion to her.

Lena didn't need constant engagement to feel secure. She often felt safest in stillness, in space. She could feel Jack's emotional charge coming before he even opened his mouth, the tone, the edge, the question disguised as challenge. And in that split second, she would assess: Was this worth engaging in? Or was this just Jack trying to stir the pot?

Sometimes, she fired back. Sometimes, she laughed. Sometimes, she ignored it altogether. It depended on the day, and on how much energy she had left.

To Jack, her resistance was proof she could hold her own.

To Lena, his persistence was exhausting.

This wasn't emotional immaturity. It wasn't about who cared more. It was about survival instincts. About two people with the same fear responding in opposing ways, each believing the other had the upper hand.

When Connection Feels Like Combat

Over time, their interactions settled into a rhythm, one that neither of them liked, but both of them recognized:

- Jack would poke the bear. He'd challenge Lena, push a boundary, make a remark he knew might land wrong, anything to keep the air from going still.
- Lena would hold her ground, sometimes playfully, sometimes wearily, but if she sensed that Jack was pressing just to provoke, she'd disengage.
- Jack would escalate. The more she withdrew, the more desperate he became to pull her back in. He'd sharpen his tone, dig deeper, say something reckless.

- Lena would walk away, not as punishment, but as self-preservation. If she couldn't win the game, she refused to play.

And yet, this wasn't static. Over time, especially during extended periods of stress, the roles reversed.

There were times when Lena pursued. She wasn't trying to provoke, but to understand. She asked the hard questions. She demanded clarity. She wanted answers, connection, repair. And Jack, whose armor had once been made of confrontation, now found himself avoiding the conversation entirely.

Jack would go quiet. Sidestep. Detach.

Lena would press, not because she wanted a fight, but because silence, after everything, made her feel like she wasn't worth having the answer.

This flip wasn't a betrayal of character. It was the truth of fearful-avoidant attachment. When threatened, Jack fought to stay in control. When depleted, he escaped to avoid collapse. Lena, in contrast, learned to retreat early, but when emotionally cornered, she pursued out of desperation to regain footing.

They weren't rigid roles. They were reactive systems, switching, compensating, reaching, pulling.

Neither of them trusted peace. Not really. Because peace had always felt like the calm before something worse.

What This Says About Conflict-Driven Relationships

Jack and Lena's relationship was a question of how that love was sustained. Jack wanted engagement, but he didn't know how to reach for it without using tension as the vehicle. Lena wanted security, but her version of security required control over her own emotional energy, and Jack's methods often violated that boundary.

Conflict became the language they both understood. While often productive, it was familiar.

This is why high-conflict relationships don't always break from the weight of fighting itself. They break from fatigue, when one or both partners stop having the strength to keep engaging the same way.

Their pattern wasn't about who was wrong. It was about who moved first. Who pushed, who resisted, and when the script flipped.

Jack wanted emotional presence.

Lena wanted emotional safety.

But the ways they went about getting those things often worked directly against each other.

What Comes Next

Attachment theory explains why Jack and Lena's relationship was so charged, but it also exposes why their dynamic was so volatile. Their need for closeness wasn't the problem. Their fear of closeness was.

Some partners fight to confirm that they still exist in the relationship. Some chase because silence feels like rejection. And still others withdraw because they've run out of safe ways to respond.

Which brings us to the next chapter.

When does engagement-seeking become a form of connection, and when does it become control?

When does emotional presence become emotional pressure?

In Chapter 3, we'll explore the function of provocation, how partners like Jack "poke the bear" not to destroy connection, but to keep it alive. And how, over time, that strategy becomes a slow kind of erosion neither partner sees coming.

Chapter Three

Engagement-Seeking Behavior – Why Some People Poke the Bear

Love is not always expressed through tenderness. For some, connection is forged in friction, through challenge, provocation, or emotional collision. This is the engine behind engagement-seeking behavior, where one partner instigates conflict to keep the relationship alive.

It may look like sabotage, but it often comes from a desperate need to stay relevant, to avoid being emotionally left behind.

Why Some People Poke the Bear

Some partners don't wait for affection. They provoke it. Engagement-seeking is often misunderstood because it doesn't arrive as vulnerability, it arrives as pressure. Teasing, baiting, arguing. Button-pushing that feels unnecessary, even aggressive, to the one on the receiving end. But for the instigator, it's a way to maintain presence, to confirm the emotional tether is still intact.

This is not about curiosity, it's about control.

For someone like Jack, engagement isn't a gentle bid for closeness. It's a power-preservation mechanism. When Lena pulls away or emotionally disengages, Jack feels himself slipping, like a man grasping at smoke. He escalates not to win the fight, but to stop the fading. If teasing won't work, provocation will. If words won't land, volume will.

If he can't inspire affection, he'll provoke resistance. Either way, she'll have to respond.

Jack doesn't just want to know if Lena is present, he needs confirmation that he still matters. When he teases her, it's not lighthearted. It's strategic. If she bites back, even playfully, the connection is alive. But if she ignores him, if she disengages, he sharpens his edge. A joke becomes a dare. A dare becomes a threat.

And that threat is clear: I will escalate until you respond.

Lena recognizes the pattern. She knows that engaging will only feed the cycle, but ignoring him won't end it, it will accelerate it. Jack doesn't test for reassurance. He provokes to demand it. He won't ask, "Are we okay?" He'll push until her resistance confirms she's still in the ring.

And if conflict is the only way to get that confirmation, so be it.

Maintaining Presence: When Closeness Becomes Coercion

Jack doesn't start fights because he wants to hurt Lena. He starts fights because he refuses to be invisible. Her silence, intentional or not, triggers a spiral. He begins to imagine a version of reality where he no longer matters. That fear makes him dangerous.

He starts small. A tease. A sarcastic jab. A comment just sharp enough to get under her skin. If she doesn't react, he raises the stakes. He doesn't need her to smile. He just needs her to flinch.

He doesn't want calm. Calm feels like absence. Conflict, even chaotic, confirms that something between them is still alive, and that he's still part of it.

Lena, on the other hand, sees the same moment differently. She's not withholding to punish him, she's protecting herself. What Jack calls passion, she experiences as pressure. Every jab forces her to choose: engage and lose emotional safety, or disengage and risk escalation.

She doesn't want to fight, but Jack won't let her opt out. And the more he demands presence, the more she retreats. She isn't indifferent, but his version of closeness feels like a trap.

Jack fears irrelevance. Lena fears entrapment. And this is where love turns into war.

Emotional Expression as a Substitute for Vulnerability

Jack doesn't say, "I feel disconnected." He doesn't say, "I'm scared you're drifting." And when he does say "I need you," it's a call for physical intimacy, not emotional transparency. What he's really asking for stays buried under sarcasm and sharpness.

Instead of voicing vulnerability, he pokes.

He teases her values. He challenges her tone. He makes some offhand comment that forces her to look up, to respond, to see him again. Because that's the goal, not resolution. Just re-engagement.

Lena knows the pattern. When Jack starts probing, she knows it's not really about her opinion or her mood. It's about his rising anxiety. But she's done being baited into emotional caretaking. She won't unravel every jab to find the need underneath. That's not her job.

If he's taking his day out on her, she won't play along.

Jack escalates because it works. Not always, but often enough to reinforce the pattern. The moment Lena fires back, even in irritation, he breathes easier. The connection is restored, not peaceful, but active. And active feels better than absent.

But it comes at a cost.

Lena doesn't experience these moments as connection. She sees them as compulsion disguised as affection. And the more Jack demands interaction without emotional accountability, the more she hardens. She will not be dragged into closeness against her will.

Because the line between pursuit and coercion is crossed the moment engagement becomes nonconsensual.

Coercion Disguised as Closeness

Engagement-seeking isn't always about immaturity or a need for attention. Sometimes, it's about survival. Jack doesn't provoke Lena because he enjoys conflict, he provokes her because conflict is the last reliable way he knows to feel connected. But that need, unchecked, becomes a weapon.

What begins as a bid for presence turns into a test of dominance: Will you still look at me if I make you angry? Will you still answer if I won't let you leave?

This isn't harmless tension. It's not romantic friction. It's control with a softer mask.

Jack isn't just poking the bear. He's trying to keep the bear awake, engaged, emotionally active, because silence feels like disappearance. He fears becoming irrelevant, unseen, emotionally erased.

But Lena doesn't fear absence. She fears captivity. She resents the forced intimacy, the emotional debt she didn't agree to incur. She withholds, not to hurt Jack, but to preserve herself.

This is the heart of their dynamic: Jack fights for connection at all costs, while Lena measures the cost and quietly decides what she's willing to pay.

The challenge isn't to eliminate engagement-seeking, it's to understand when it's a plea, and when it's a demand. When it's a bid for closeness, and when it's coercion.

And in the moments when it becomes coercion, the question isn't just "Will she stay engaged?"

It's "Should she?"

Case Study: The Different Faces of Engagement-Seeking

Engagement-seeking doesn't look the same in every relationship. It's not one behavior, it's a pattern, shaped by attachment wounds, stress responses, and the emotional currency of the relationship itself. For some, it stays in the realm of banter and play. But for others, like Jack, it mutates into something heavier. Something that walks and talks like connection, but feels like pressure to the one on the receiving end.

Jack doesn't just seek engagement. He ensures it. And when that doesn't work, he demands it.

The push-pull between them plays out in different forms. Sometimes it starts with teasing, Jack's idea of foreplay, tension, presence. He thrives on the spark, the sharp edge of witty back-and-forth that makes them feel, for a moment, like they're on the same team again. If Lena jabs back, he lights up. But if her response is dull, if she disengages, he doesn't accept it as a limit.

He pushes harder.

What starts as banter becomes bait. He prods, pokes, says something just pointed enough to force her back into the ring. But what happens when that fails? When the jokes don't land, when the tension doesn't spark, when Lena simply refuses to bite?

That's when Jack shifts. What once looked like need now looks like domination.

He tells himself it's not about control. He's not trying to overpower her. He just needs her to respond. Because her silence, her calm, her distance, feels like he's disappearing. Like the connection itself is dissolving beneath his feet. That's when the real escalation starts.

If sarcasm doesn't work, he ups the voltage. His comments get sharper. His voice gets louder. His physical presence looms larger. He doesn't want a fight, but if a fight is what it takes to feel real again, he'll go there. His fear of becoming invisible is driving him forward.

But Lena doesn't see fear. She sees pressure. A forced emotional contract she never agreed to. A relational trap disguised as need.

What Jack experiences as desperation, Lena experiences as invasion.

Not all engagement-seeking is playful. Not all of it is even about connection. For some, it's about restoring a sense of control when life feels unmanageable. Conflict becomes the outlet. Tension becomes the coping mechanism. And the relationship becomes the place where that chaos gets dumped.

Jack doesn't always know he's doing it. If something unsettles him, stress at work, unresolved shame, fear he won't name, it shows up in how he engages Lena. Rather than becoming vulnerable, he applies pressure with provocation. He doesn't say, "I'm spiraling." He doesn't say, "I feel powerless." Instead, he zeroes in on her.

If she's quiet, he makes noise. If she's calm, he stirs the pot. If she disengages, he triggers the one thing guaranteed to bring her back, conflict.

Because that always works.

If he jokes and she ignores him, he raises the stakes. If he challenges her and she brushes it off, he sharpens the accusation. If all else fails, he taps into the part of himself he knows she can't ignore, his anger.

Because when he escalates, she always shows up.

That's the rhythm. That's the cycle. It doesn't matter how tired she is, or how many times she's said no. Jack knows, consciously or not, that his escalation has power. And Lena knows it too.

He calls it love. She experiences it as emotional siege.

What looks like connection to Jack feels like entrapment to Lena. And neither of them has the language to name the difference.

Where It Becomes a Problem

Jack tells himself he's reacting to Lena's distance. But what he's really doing is preserving power. When she doesn't respond, he doesn't reflect, he escalates. He pushes until withdrawal becomes impossible, until she either fights back or gives in.

The teasing that once passed as flirtation becomes an interrogation. The emotional pokes become pointed, deliberate, inescapable. He isn't just seeking connection anymore. He's eliminating the option of silence.

For Lena, it's a no-win situation. If she engages, she reinforces the cycle. If she withdraws, she triggers his fury. Her boundaries don't just get tested, they get trampled. The space she needs to feel safe becomes something Jack refuses to allow.

And so their relationship becomes a negotiation of pressure. Jack demands presence. Lena resists the terms. But in the end, she's left with only two options: comply, or endure the consequences of disengaging.

Key Takeaway

Engagement-seeking can be a relational lifeline, until it becomes a trap. Jack frames his behavior as a response to Lena's detachment, but in reality, it's an attempt to override her autonomy. It stops being about connection the moment Lena isn't allowed to choose it.

For high-conflict couples like Jack and Lena, the solution isn't compromise. It's clarity. True connection cannot be coerced. If emotional presence is extracted through pressure, it isn't connection, it's captivity.

Final Thoughts: Recognizing the Different Faces of Engagement-Seeking

Jack's behavior isn't just a quirk. It isn't harmless. And it isn't always conscious. But it is strategic.

When Lena disengages, he escalates. If she ignores his teasing, he corners her with sharper words. If she stays silent, he raises his voice. If she walks away, he follows. He doesn't stop until her silence is broken.

To Jack, this feels like fighting for love. To Lena, it feels like being hunted.

This is where engagement-seeking stops being a dynamic and starts being a danger.

Understanding the difference isn't just about semantics, it's about survival. Because when one partner's need for connection overrides the other's right to disengage, the question isn't whether they'll keep fighting.

It's whether they'll survive the fight at all.

How Childhood Dynamics Influence Engagement-Seeking in Adulthood

Engagement-seeking doesn't appear out of nowhere. It's not a personality glitch or a spontaneous quirk, it's learned. Conditioned. Practiced. And it often starts long before the word "relationship" means anything at all.

Children raised in emotionally volatile homes don't learn that connection is built, they learn that connection is provoked. If a parent only responds when something explodes, the child learns to light the match. They don't seek affection through calm, they stir conflict to get a reaction. Because even a negative reaction is proof of presence.

That pattern doesn't vanish in adulthood. It matures. It refines. But it doesn't disappear.

Some of the most common foundations of engagement-seeking include:

- *Unpredictable Attention* – When connection was inconsistent, children learned that provocation was the surest way to secure engagement. As adults, they associate conflict with visibility.
- *Instability as Passion* – In homes where emotional highs and lows were the norm, regulation feels foreign. Calm is interpreted as detachment. Volatility is mistaken for love.
- *Conflict as Connection* – When bonding happened through debate or tension, emotional safety becomes synonymous with emotional friction. Peace feels like distance. Tension feels like presence.

For Jack, the conditioning ran deep. In a house full of siblings where noise was constant and attention was rationed, the only way to carve out space was to push back. Conflict wasn't affection, but it was acknowledgment. If someone challenged you, it meant you hadn't disappeared.

Lena's upbringing taught her the opposite. Silence wasn't neglect, it was safety. Emotional stillness was protection. Escalation was the thing to avoid at all costs. She read tone like other kids read bedtime stories. She tracked volume, posture, and exit routes. In her world, retreat was survival.

So when Jack teased her, it didn't register as play. It registered as pressure. And when he escalated? That wasn't passion, it was a trap.

They weren't just clashing personalities. They were enacting blueprints. His fear of fading met her fear of being cornered. And between them, conflict wasn't just a pattern.

It was a reenactment of everything they never chose, but couldn't stop repeating.

The Emotional Toll of Engagement-Seeking

Engagement-seeking often masquerades as charm, intensity, or passion, but its impact depends entirely on how it lands. What one partner experiences as electricity, the other may experience as emotional demand. For some, it energizes. For others, it drains.

Psychologists have identified three common responses to this dynamic (Pietromonaco & Powers, 2015):

- *Reciprocal Engagement* – When both partners enjoy emotional sparring, it can fuel connection.
- *Emotional Exhaustion* – When the engagement feels one-sided or relentless, the receiving partner begins to pull away, not out of indifference, but from depletion.
- *Avoidance and Shutdown* – When the provocation becomes intolerable, the partner may disengage entirely, triggering breakdowns in communication.

For Lena, her response depended on her internal bandwidth. Some days, she had the energy to meet Jack's sharpness with her own. Other days, she couldn't absorb one more emotional jab. On those days, Jack's teasing didn't feel like a bid for playfulness, it felt like pressure wrapped in expectation.

And expectation, for someone like Lena, has always been a warning sign.

This is the rift inside high-conflict dynamics. One partner thrives on tension as evidence of love. The other interprets that same tension as a signal to retreat. Without awareness and adjustment, the very energy intended to connect becomes the force that slowly wears the relationship down.

The Psychology of Engagement-Seeking

At its core, engagement-seeking is both behavioral and biological. It's rooted in early experience, yes, but it's also reinforced by nervous system sensitivity, emotional reactivity, and unconscious regulation strategies (Mikulincer & Shaver, 2016).

For someone like Jack, engagement isn't just a habit, it's a way to anchor himself emotionally. When the room feels too quiet or Lena feels too distant, he doesn't just notice the shift, he feels it as a threat. Stirring conflict isn't about creating chaos, it's about avoiding disappearance.

And it works. Conflict brings presence. Presence brings relief.

This pattern is often reinforced by what happens after the conflict. Studies show that post-conflict bonding, soothing, reconnecting, the emotional makeup scene, can make the brain link tension with intimacy (Taylor et al., 2000).

For Jack, the fight is just the path. The resolution is the reward. Even when escalation hurts them both, the quiet afterward tells him he hasn't been abandoned.

Lena doesn't experience it that way. She doesn't chase emotional restoration. She guards against emotional invasion. Where Jack seeks intensity, she seeks control.

Engagement-Seeking and Relationship Longevity

It's tempting to assume that high-conflict couples are less stable, but research complicates that assumption. In some relationships, friction isn't just tolerable, it's sustaining. Couples who use intellectual challenge, teasing, and playful tension as part of their relational language often report stronger emotional investment and longer-term passion (Huston & Melz, 2004).

But the key difference is how that engagement is used.

When tension remains constructive, playful, mutual, bounded by trust, it can energize connection. But when it escalates into criticism, control, or emotional threat, it corrodes the foundation it was meant to reinforce (Gottman & Levenson, 2000).

It's not the conflict itself that's damaging, it's when the conflict becomes a tool. A lever. A test.

How Engagement-Seeking Helps Regulate Emotions

Jack doesn't pick fights to entertain himself. He does it because conflict offers something he can't seem to get any other way: emotional proof.

When he's unsure of his footing, stressed, rejected, ashamed, he stirs interaction. It soothes him. It gives him something to hold onto when his internal world feels slippery. And without realizing it, he uses their dynamic to regulate emotions he doesn't know how to name.

Engagement-seeking offers:

- *External Validation* – Provoking Lena confirms that he still has a place in her emotional world.
- *Emotional Distraction* – Conflict gives him something immediate to manage, diverting his focus from internal distress.
- *Adrenaline and Control* – The physical rush of escalation creates a temporary sense of power when vulnerability feels dangerous (Koole, 2009).

Jack doesn't consciously think, I'll pick a fight so I don't have to feel this ache in my chest. But that's exactly what's happening.

When Engagement is a Test

Engagement-seeking can look like a game. But sometimes, it's a test, one the other partner doesn't know they're taking.

Jack doesn't walk around consciously thinking, If she loves me, she'll fight back. But that's the emotional subtext. If Lena engages, even in anger, he's reassured. If she doesn't, he spirals.

And so he sets the stage. He pushes. He pokes. He waits.

Because silence is more threatening than rejection. A fight means she's still emotionally invested. Indifference would mean he's lost her.

Learned Patterns of Engagement-Seeking

These dynamics don't form in adulthood. They are rehearsed in childhood, coded into nervous systems that learned early how to survive love that wasn't steady.

Studies show that when caregivers are most responsive during moments of emotional intensity, crying, yelling, acting out, children internalize a pattern: big emotions get attention. Calm does not (Cassidy & Berlin, 1994).

Jack didn't decide one day to pick fights instead of expressing need. He learned that intensity equals engagement. That escalation is the fastest route to presence. And that the quiet moments in between, the ones that might feel safe to someone else, signaled abandonment to him.

Lena learned the opposite. High emotional intensity wasn't presence, it was chaos. It meant someone was about to lose control. She adapted by pulling back, minimizing her responses, and staying one step ahead of the emotional current. If she could retreat early enough, maybe she could avoid the flood.

Neither of them was wrong. But they were catastrophically mismatched.

The more Jack escalated, the more Lena disappeared. The more Lena withdrew, the more Jack panicked. And between them, love became something neither could hold onto without hurting the other.

Jack wanted proof that he mattered. Lena wanted proof that she was still free.

And as long as escalation was the only thing that confirmed connection, they'd remain locked in a dynamic where presence was purchased at the cost of peace.

The Psychological Costs of Unchecked Engagement-Seeking

Engagement-seeking can keep a relationship emotionally alive, but when one partner keeps pressing and the other starts to retreat, it becomes something else entirely. What begins as spark or banter can morph into exhaustion. Trust corrodes. Emotional safety cracks. Eventually, even affection feels like pressure.

And the more one partner escalates to preserve presence, the more the other resists to preserve autonomy.

This is the high cost of unchecked engagement-seeking: a relational rhythm that looks like connection from the outside but feels like erosion on the inside.

1. **Emotional Fatigue: The Cost of Constant Provocation**

For partners like Lena, the demand to stay emotionally "on" becomes unsustainable. Jack's pursuit isn't always cruel, but it's constant. Some days, she meets it with her own fire. Other days, it feels like being poked by someone who refuses to read the room.

The difference lies in consent. When she chooses to engage, it's connection. When Jack demands it, especially when she's tired, raw, or guarded, it feels like coercion in disguise.

The problem isn't just the teasing. It's the assumption behind it: If I provoke you, you'll have to respond.

But Lena doesn't owe her presence. And when Jack treats engagement like an entitlement, she experiences it as intrusion.

2. **The Loss of Emotional Safety**

When engagement becomes proof that you care, evidence that you're still in, it stops feeling like connection and starts feeling like surveillance. Jack doesn't always recognize what he's doing. But when he escalates after Lena pulls away, it's not because he wants closeness. It's because he refuses to feel irrelevant.

And in that refusal, he starts to override her boundaries.

Every withdrawal becomes a threat to Jack's internal equilibrium. And every escalation becomes Lena's punishment for choosing space.

What began as relational friction now functions as a power struggle. Jack is fighting to be seen. Lena is fighting not to be cornered.

3. **Escalation and Relationship Burnout**

When neither partner interrupts the pattern, provocation becomes default. Jack escalates reflexively. Lena withdraws instinctively. Arguments start without cause. Tension simmers even in silence.

And over time, the fight becomes less about what's said, and more about who refuses to back down.

For Jack and Lena, the turning point wasn't mutual understanding, it was mutual depletion. Jack had to recognize that not every pause was abandonment. Lena had to recognize that not all provocation was manipulation. But even awareness isn't a cure. Without new behaviors, recognition is just another step in the cycle.

When Engagement-Seeking Becomes a Strain

Engagement-seeking can be electrifying, when it's mutual. When both partners understand the rhythm and want to stay in the dance, it becomes a source of connection, even fun.

But when one partner feels trapped in a loop of provocation and response, it stops being energizing. It starts feeling like warfare.

What keeps Jack emotionally anchored can leave Lena emotionally depleted. His escalation is meant to tether them together. But from her side, it feels like he's pulling the rope tighter each time she tries to breathe.

Signs That Engagement-Seeking Is Doing More Harm Than Good

- *Emotional Burnout* – When the energy that once sparked connection now drains it.
- *Escalation Beyond Playfulness* – Teasing that shifts into contempt, criticism, or emotional attacks.
- *No Room for Repair* – Conflict that never closes. Resentment becomes sediment.
- *Feeling Tested Instead of Loved* – When every disengagement feels like failing a hidden test.

Lena could feel the shift. Some days, Jack's poking felt like a sideways kind of intimacy, a sharp but familiar dance. Other days, it felt like she was being asked to show up when she had nothing left to give.

She started reading his jabs like emotional barometers. Sometimes, they said "Do you still care?" Other times, they said "You don't get to leave me here alone."

And that second one wasn't a question. It was a demand.

Because at some point, the line between teasing and coercion disappears, not because it was never there, but because one partner keeps stepping over it.

The Difference Between Engagement and Manipulation

Not all provocation comes from love. Sometimes it comes from fear, fear of abandonment, fear of powerlessness, fear of emotional irrelevance. And when that fear isn't named, it starts shaping behavior in destructive ways.

When Jack provokes to force Lena's reaction, he's not always aware of what he's doing. But intention doesn't erase impact.

So how do you tell the difference?

- *Intent Matters* – If the goal is connection, the behavior remains tethered to love. If the goal is control, the line has already been crossed.
- *Emotional Safety* – Engagement invites expression. Manipulation punishes it.
- *Who Benefits?* – Real connection serves both partners. Coercion serves only the one who fears being left behind.

Lena understood the nuance. Jack's teasing wasn't always easy to absorb, but she knew when it was about staying close and when it was about staying in control. If he had ever turned it into emotional leverage, to make her question herself, to chip away at her confidence, she wouldn't have stayed.

But staying didn't mean it wasn't costing her.

A relationship built on resistance can survive. It can even thrive, under the right conditions. But it only works when both partners choose the tension freely, when push and pull is a dance, not a demand.

The moment engagement becomes a test of endurance, the foundation begins to fracture.

Because a relationship held together by coercion isn't intimacy, it's containment.

And when presence is extracted through pressure, what you're left with isn't connection. It's compliance.

Jack doesn't always mean to control. But his fear of becoming irrelevant drives him to escalate. Lena doesn't always mean to reject. But her fear of losing autonomy drives her to retreat.

And when love becomes a battle between being seen and staying free, both partners end up losing.

The Spectrum of Playful and Harmful Engagement

Engagement-seeking exists on a spectrum. At one end, it's banter, sharp wit, mutual teasing, a dance of friction that keeps the relationship alive and responsive. When both partners are attuned and willing, this dynamic can feel invigorating, intimate, even joyful.

But not all engagement is welcome.

When provocation becomes persistent, when it begins to override boundaries or ignore exhaustion, it shifts. The energy that once sparked connection begins to wear. One partner keeps pushing for interaction, the other starts pulling away.

What began as affection through tension now feels like pressure wearing the other person down.

And if it escalates further, provocation becomes a tool of control. The goal isn't connection anymore, it's dominance. One partner needs proof they still matter. The other no longer gets to choose when or how they engage.

This is the dark end of the spectrum: when the emotional stakes of not responding feel higher than the cost of staying silent.

For Jack, escalation wasn't always a decision. It was a defense, an instinctive attempt to preserve emotional relevance. For Lena, resistance wasn't just frustration, it was self-protection. And when presence is forced, not chosen, even closeness feels like captivity.

Cultural Perspectives on Engagement-Seeking

Not every culture frames emotional engagement the same way. In some contexts, sharpness is affection. In others, it's aggression.

In many Western cultures, like the U.S., Canada, or Australia, verbal engagement is often seen as a sign of passion, truth-telling, and even romantic spark. A good fight can feel like proof that the relationship is alive. In Eastern cultures, such as Japan, South Korea, or China, harmony is more highly valued. Conflict is avoided out of respect, and teasing may be interpreted as rude.

Even within cultures, gender roles shape expectations. In some environments, men are conditioned to initiate tension, while women are expected to absorb or de-escalate it. In others, particularly in high-intensity cultures like parts of Latin America or the Mediterranean, emotional fire is part of the dance. Love is loud.

Jack and Lena carried all of this, consciously or not. They weren't just navigating each other, they were carrying histories, norms, temperaments, and trauma.

Had they grown up in a home or culture where restraint was the marker of intimacy, things might have unfolded differently. But they didn't.

Their version of love came with sparks. And sometimes those sparks lit fires that neither of them meant to start.

How Personality Traits Influence Engagement-Seeking

Engagement-seeking isn't just a product of childhood or culture. It's also tied to temperament, who we are, how we're wired, and what emotional conditions we gravitate toward. Some people find stability in steadiness. Others find it in contrast, in stimulation, in that energetic tug-of-war that keeps things moving.

Research on personality theory, particularly the Big Five model, sheds light on who's more likely to use provocation as engagement (McCrae & Costa, 1999):

• *High Extraversion* – Extroverts often thrive on stimulation and feedback. They may seek emotional exchange the way others seek quiet, needing it to feel grounded.

• *High Openness to Experience* – Those with high openness often use intellectual challenge and debate as tools for intimacy. It's not conflict, it's curiosity.

- *Low Agreeableness* – Individuals low in agreeableness may naturally challenge others, not to hurt, but to engage. They're less comfortable with harmony that feels stagnant.
- *High Neuroticism* – People high in neuroticism often seek emotional reassurance, and conflict becomes a backdoor route to getting it. *If you're fighting with me, you're still here.*
- *Conscientiousness* – Those with lower conscientiousness are more likely to act impulsively and have poor self-regulation, which can amplify reactive engagement. This trait is less predictive than others like extraversion or neuroticism.

Jack was wired for engagement. Provocation wasn't just a coping mechanism, it was part of his nature. He came alive in debate, in contrast, in heat. He pushed Lena not just to connect, but to see if she was still there.

Lena could match him when she wanted to. Her mind was sharp, her tongue sharper. But sparring wasn't her home base. She needed more quiet. She needed to know that love didn't always have to come with impact. That she didn't have to brace for it.

Their friction wasn't just about disagreement, it was about the terms of safety. What Jack needed to feel seen was what Lena avoided to stay whole.

The Impact of Stress and External Factors on Engagement-Seeking

Engagement-seeking doesn't just show up when relationships are strained, it often intensifies when external pressure mounts.

Work stress, financial instability, unresolved personal pain, these things create emotional noise. And when that noise gets too loud internally, some people redirect it externally. Conflict becomes the volume knob they can control.

Jack never said, "Work was brutal today, and I feel powerless." He said something snide instead. He poked at Lena's logic. He made a comment he knew would get a rise. He wasn't looking for a fight, but fighting in this moment felt more manageable than drowning. He was looking for grounding.

Lena, however, didn't care why he was poking. It still hurt. It still felt like she was being drawn into emotional labor she hadn't agreed to perform. And by the time she realized the tension wasn't about her, the damage had already been done.

Understanding the source of engagement-seeking, whether internal stress or unresolved fear, doesn't excuse it. But it can shift how we respond.

Because sometimes the conflict isn't about the relationship at all. It's about needing somewhere to put the ache.

How Childhood Dynamics Influence Engagement-Seeking

Engagement-seeking starts early. Before it becomes a strategy, it's a survival instinct.

In homes where affection came unpredictably, children learned to provoke in order to stay visible. If calm brought distance and noise brought attention, the lesson was simple: make noise. Be loud. Be sharp. Be impossible to ignore.

For Jack, that lesson stuck. His childhood wasn't tender, it was tense. Love didn't whisper. It tested. And so he became someone who tested back.

He didn't ask Lena for reassurance. He challenged her. He pressed until she responded. He needed confirmation that she knew he was still there.

Lena, on the other hand, learned to survive by vanishing. When emotions ran high in her home, it meant danger. Not engagement. Not intimacy. Just volatility and fallout. She learned to read the warning signs and step back early. Quiet wasn't detachment, it was control.

So while Jack escalated to stay emotionally present, Lena withdrew to stay emotionally safe.

And the more Jack pushed, the more Lena disappeared. The more Lena retreated, the harder Jack fought to bring her back.

And whether they could ever stop the cycle without breaking the relationship altogether was still an open question.

A Reflection on the Foundations of Friction

When you push, what are you really trying to hold onto?

When you pull away, what are you trying to protect?

Engagement-seeking is rarely about the surface interaction. It's about survival strategies woven into us long before we had language for them. Some provoke to feel seen. Others retreat to stay safe. Neither instinct is random. Neither comes without cost.

Before we can manage tension, we have to recognize what it's doing for us, and what it's costing us.

So ask yourself:
- Do I seek engagement to connect, or to avoid disappearing?
- Do I withdraw to find calm, or to avoid surrendering control?
- When I provoke, is it an invitation, or an ultimatum?
- When I resist, is it boundary or fear?

This isn't the part where you fix anything. This is the part where you tell the truth about the game you've been playing, and whether either of you ever agreed to the rules.

Before you can change a dynamic, you have to understand why you're still participating in it.

Before you can stop the cycle, you have to admit you're in one.

And that's where we go next.

PART II: Navigating the Highs and Lows

Journey into the volatile heart of the relationship where boundaries blur, power struggles peak, and danger quietly enters the room.

Chapter Four

Control vs. Autonomy – The Fine Line Between Disengagement & Dismissal

Lena's Survival Mechanism: The Art of Disengagement

Lena had spent years learning when to push and when to disappear. Some fights weren't worth the energy. Some arguments weren't meant to be won. And some moments were about survival, not resolution.

Her childhood taught her that engagement could be dangerous. The louder she argued, the more likely she was to lose control of the situation, and herself. Defiance only prolonged what was coming. Explanation only made her seem defensive.

The only thing that worked, the only thing that ever made the chaos stop, was silence.

So she shut down.

She pulled back. She stayed still until the emotional weather changed. What started as instinct became discipline. Not everything warranted her engagement. Not every emotional demand deserved her energy.

As an adult, this coping strategy took on new names. She called it "creating space," or "taking a step back." Others called it avoidance. Fine. She didn't care. She wasn't walking away from problems, she was walking away from escalation. That distinction mattered.

Disengagement was how she stayed in control of herself. In a situation where she couldn't control anyone else, especially someone like Jack, pulling inward was how she avoided being overrun. She didn't argue her way to safety. She didn't fight her way to peace. She survived by knowing when to stop talking.

Not every fight required retreat. Some just needed silence. If she gave Jack enough space to vent, he usually calmed down. It wasn't about letting him win. It was about letting the fire burn itself out. She didn't add oxygen to something already blazing. She didn't tell him he was right. She didn't tell him he was wrong. She just disengaged.

And it worked. At first.

But when the intensity grew, when Jack wouldn't let her step back, wouldn't let her go quiet, wouldn't let the moment breathe, her strategy had to evolve. Disengagement wasn't enough. She had to get out.

There was a difference between shutting down and walking away. Between going still and going silent. Most people didn't notice it. Jack certainly didn't. But Lena did. One was about self-regulation. The other was about escape.

Disengagement was the first line of defense. Retreat was the last.

Psychologists have studied avoidant coping strategies in high-conflict relationships. It's common for individuals with trauma histories to disengage not because they don't care, but because emotional conflict feels unsafe. Avoidance, in that context, isn't apathy, it's regulation (Kashdan, Barrios, Forsyth, & Steger, 2014). It allows the overwhelmed individual to maintain emotional stability without being consumed by someone else's volatility. In emotionally charged relationships, that survival instinct doesn't disappear. It gets repackaged as strategy.

Lena didn't disengage to win. She disengaged to preserve.

Disengagement, when effective, kept her grounded. Retreat, when necessary, kept her sane. But it also fed the cycle.

To Jack, silence wasn't space. It was rejection. He didn't hear quiet as de-escalation. He heard it as abandonment. Disengagement wasn't something he understood. If he was still in it, the other person should be, too. That was the rule. Arguments ended when he was ready for them to end, when they had been "finished," as if resolution were something you could force into place by sheer volume.

Jack didn't always chase. But when he did, it was because her withdrawal lit up every nerve that told him he was being erased. He didn't need to be agreed with. He didn't need her to concede. He just needed to know she was still in the conversation. Still tethered to it. Still tethered to him.

When she pulled away, he felt it like disconnection. Like irrelevance.

Their dynamic mirrored what psychologists refer to as demand-withdraw conflict: one partner presses, the other retreats. The more one demands engagement, the more the other distances. And round and round it goes (Christensen & Heavey, 1990). The tragedy of the pattern is that both people believe they're protecting something. Jack was protecting the relationship by not letting it go unresolved. Lena was protecting the relationship by not letting it go up in flames.

Neither approach felt like abandonment to the one doing it. But both felt like betrayal to the one on the receiving end.

Jack wasn't afraid Lena would leave. He was afraid she would leave him out. That she would make a decision about the relationship without including him in it. That she would go quiet and not come back until it suited her, and then pretend the silence never happened. For someone like Jack, whose presence had always been tied to influence, whose voice had always been his anchor, being ignored wasn't just aggravating. It was destabilizing.

When Lena disengaged, she wasn't avoiding Jack. She was avoiding the loss of herself.

When Jack escalated, he wasn't trying to dominate her. He was trying not to disappear.

The more she pulled back, the more he pushed. The more he pushed, the more she needed distance. What started as a moment of disconnect could easily spiral into something larger. Not because either of them wanted it to, but because neither of them could tolerate the other's instinct.

Jack needed movement. Lena needed stillness.

Jack needed answers. Lena needed space.

Jack needed connection. Lena needed control.

And neither of them knew how to get what they needed without making the other feel violated.

Jack's Reaction: The Urgency to Be Heard

Jack had never been good at waiting.

Silence unsettled him. Distance felt like punishment. He didn't fear Lena leaving forever, but he hated the way she could shut him out like flipping a switch. The way she could disengage so easily, like the conversation hadn't mattered at all.

He didn't need to win. He just needed to finish.

Some arguments lasted minutes. Some stretched for hours. But no matter how long it took, Jack could push through the fight as long as he knew it was going somewhere. As long as he knew Lena was still in it with him.

But when she disengaged? When she shut down completely?

That was when the frustration turned sharp. That was when he felt it slip, not her, but his grasp on the moment, his influence over it. That was what he couldn't handle. Not the space itself, but the lack of control over what happened inside it.

Jack saw disengagement as avoidance. As an easy way out. He knew what silence did. It killed momentum. It let emotions settle, made people second-guess their own anger. That was the trick, wasn't it? Let it die in the air so it never had to be addressed. He wasn't stupid. He saw what she was doing.

What he didn't see was how different it looked from Lena's side.

He thought she was escaping accountability. She thought she was avoiding escalation. He thought she was shutting him out to hurt him. She thought she was shutting down to protect herself. They were both convinced they understood the situation. They were both wrong.

Jack believed Lena used silence as a weapon, when in reality, it was a shield.

Psychologists studying high-intensity relationships note that conflict-driven individuals like Jack often perceive disengagement as a power play rather than a regulatory strategy (Simpson & Overall, 2013). They believe the partner withdrawing is trying to control the situation through avoidance, when, in reality, the withdrawal is an act of emotional self-preservation.

Jack didn't see Lena's retreat as a boundary. He saw it as a game.

And if that was the game? He refused to lose.

Jack's instinct had always been engagement. If there was a problem, talk it out. If the conversation was unfinished, finish it. If something felt unresolved, keep pushing until there was closure.

If she walked away, that closure was stolen from him.

That's why he followed. Why he pressed. Why he knocked on doors, asked more questions, refused to let things sit in unresolved silence. That's why, even when he told himself to back off, he rarely did.

Research on engagement-driven partners in conflict cycles suggests that people who feel ignored in moments of high stress escalate their behavior to force a response (Christensen & Heavey, 1990). It's not necessarily about manipulation, often, it's about deep discomfort with uncertainty.

That's where Jack lived.

He didn't fear abandonment, but he feared irrelevance. If Lena controlled when and how the fight ended, then she was dictating the terms of their connection.

Jack didn't believe one person should have that power.

When Lena disengaged, he felt like his presence had been revoked. Like he had lost his place in the conversation. And if he lost his place in the conversation, how far was that from losing his place in her life?

He never said that part out loud.

Because he didn't really believe that Lena would leave him, not in the permanent, world-ending way that people talk about abandonment. That wasn't what was happening here.

But this? This was still her decision.

Not his.

Jack could start a fight. But he couldn't end one. Not unless she let him.

And that made him crazy.

There were rules to a fight. A back-and-forth. A push and pull. One person spoke, the other responded. He yelled, she argued back. That was how it was supposed to work. That was how a fight ended, when it ran its course. When both people exhausted themselves enough to either resolve the issue or decide it wasn't worth it.

But when Lena walked away?

The argument ended when she decided it did.

Jack had no control over it. No say in whether it was finished. No ability to re-engage unless she let him. And that was unacceptable.

There's a concept in conflict psychology called demand-withdraw interaction, where one person pressures for engagement while the other distances themselves to self-regulate (Gottman & Levenson, 2000). The more one person pushes, the more the other withdraws. And the more the other withdraws, the more the first person escalates to force engagement.

Jack didn't think of himself as controlling.

But control wasn't always about dominance. Sometimes, it was about permission.

Who decided when they fought? Who decided when they stopped? Who dictated the terms of how and when things were resolved?

It wasn't him. And that was the problem.

He told himself he was waiting her out. Told himself he would be the bigger person, let her have her space, let her come back in her own time.

But the truth?

He was waiting for her apology.

Because that was how this worked. She left, he waited, and when she came back, things were fine, until they weren't.

Most of the time, he let it go.

But sometimes, when she acted like nothing happened, he reminded her that she owed him an apology. And when she refused, when she looked at him like he was the unreasonable one, it started all over again.

Jack had always believed that persistence was the key to fixing things. That if you just kept at it, just kept talking, just kept showing up in the moment, you could resolve anything.

Lena had learned the opposite.

She had spent her entire life knowing when to cut off the oxygen to an argument before it turned into something dangerous.

Jack's instinct was to keep going. Hers was to stop entirely.

And as long as those instincts existed in the same space, the cycle wasn't going to break.

The Fight That Keeps Repeating

There were fights Jack barely remembered, arguments that ended in silence, tension that faded on its own, moments that dissolved into nothing because neither of them had the energy to keep it going.

And then there were fights like this. The ones that stuck in the air long after the words had stopped. The ones that replayed themselves in silence, in distance, in the way she avoided looking at him when she walked into the room. These were the fights that didn't end when the yelling did.

Jack had spent too many nights waiting for something that never came. An apology. A simple admission that Lena had overreacted. That she had walked out in the middle of a conversation that still needed finishing. That she had shut him down when all he wanted was to be heard.

But Lena never apologized. Not for pulling away. Not for going silent. Not for walking out.

Because to her, she wasn't ending the conversation, she was keeping it from going somewhere worse. She was stepping back before either of them crossed a line they couldn't come back from. From her perspective, walking away was the safer option. It wasn't about control. It was about survival.

From Jack's perspective, it was all about control.

He didn't care about being right. He didn't need to win. He just needed the chance to finish the damn conversation. To have the last word, or at least a mutual one. When Lena decided she was done, that was it. There was no debate, no wrapping up, no understanding. Just silence. Just absence. And Jack couldn't stand it.

That was the pattern. He pushed. She pulled away. And in both of their minds, they were reacting to the other.

Lena saw his pressing as an attempt to manage her emotional responses, to force her to engage when she wasn't ready. Jack saw her silence as a refusal to acknowledge him. Not as a strategy. Not as self-protection. As erasure.

Neither of them could see past the immediate threat: for Lena, it was losing her autonomy. For Jack, it was losing his place in the conversation.

Psychologists call this asymmetrical conflict resolution, when one partner disengages before the other is ready, leaving the issue unresolved for one while the other moves on. The one who leaves holds the power. They decide when the fight ends, regardless of whether it feels resolved for the other person.

Jack felt that imbalance in his chest.

He wanted to feel like they were on equal footing. That if she could shut things down, then he should have some say in when things restarted. That if she walked away, she should at least acknowledge that he was still mid-sentence. But she didn't. And the longer it went on, the more it started to feel like he was waiting in a hallway for a door to open that might never unlock.

And then, somehow, she'd walk back in like nothing had happened. Like the silence had never stretched between them. Like the argument had never existed.

Most of the time, he let it go.

But sometimes, when she came back and acted like nothing had happened, he reminded her. He'd make it known, quietly, or not so quietly, that she owed him an apology. That she had left him mid-fight. That she had dictated the terms and then walked away.

And when she didn't agree, when she looked at him like he was the one making things worse, it all started again.

This wasn't a cycle of punishment and forgiveness. It wasn't even about reconciliation. It was a loop neither of them could stop because it wasn't about logic, it was about instinct. She wanted space. He wanted completion. She needed control over her level of emotional exposure. He needed control over the narrative.

Eventually, Jack stopped chasing. Not because he had changed. Not because he had learned patience or figured out how to sit in the discomfort. But because he realized that chasing didn't work. That pushing only made her dig in harder. So he stopped. He waited. And when she came back, he kept track of how long it had taken. Of how she didn't say sorry. Of how the silence was hers to initiate, but the reconnecting was somehow supposed to be mutual.

He started using her return against her.

He'd let her come back. Let her try to smooth things over. And then he'd remind her, gently or otherwise, that she had left him sitting there without resolution. That she had cut the cord and left him in the dark. That she had been the one to disappear, and now she wanted things to go back to normal like none of it mattered.

And sometimes, she let him have it. She took the blame, even if she didn't agree with it, just to keep things from spiraling again.

Other times, she refused. And when she refused, it reignited everything. Because Jack didn't just want her back. He wanted her to admit that she'd left.

What neither of them understood, what they were both too locked in to see, was that the fight wasn't about who was right. It was about who was allowed to choose when it ended.

For Jack, that choice belonged to both of them. For Lena, it was hers alone.

That difference was the fight. Every time. And neither of them knew how to surrender their part in it without losing something that felt essential.

Jack didn't stop chasing because he was growing. He stopped chasing because he had adapted. Because waiting had become the only way to stay in the game. But even as he waited, he wasn't letting go. He was collecting proof. And when she came back without apology, that proof became leverage.

The silence didn't fix anything. It just reset the loop.

Until the next time she walked away.

Until the next time he demanded something she wouldn't give.

Until the fight repeated itself again, exactly the way it always had.

Escalation: The Moment Lena Runs

Jack had blocked her path before, accidentally, without meaning to, just by the way he positioned himself when the tension climbed too high. A shift of weight in the hallway. A step too close in the middle of an argument. A tone that hardened when she turned her back. But this time, it wasn't accidental. He saw her leaving, recognized the shape of her exit before she even moved. And something in him decided: not this time.

She had already started to pull away. He could see it in her eyes, in the way her shoulders settled, not in relaxation, but in resolve. She was about to shut down. Not just quiet herself, but remove herself entirely. Her face had gone unreadable. Her arms hung loose at her sides, as if the weight of continuing was no longer hers to carry.

Jack took one step. Then another. Not aggressive. Not raised-voice angry. But sharp. Final. He was in front of her before she could move, his voice low and exact.

"We're not done."

He didn't yell. He didn't threaten. But the message was clear.

Lena's body stiffened. She didn't look at him. Didn't speak. Her breath stayed steady, but too shallow. Her hands curled into fists at her sides, and when he reached for her arms, barely touching, just enough to stop her from brushing past, she flinched.

That was the moment it shifted.

She had taken space before. Had walked out mid-sentence, gone silent for hours or even days. But this was different. She wasn't creating space. She wasn't detaching. She was preparing to run.

Fight-or-flight isn't just a theory, it's a physical truth. The body senses threat before the mind can name it. Cortisol spikes, heart rate climbs, vision narrows. Some people lean in to resolve the threat. Others get out. Lena had spent most of her life practicing control over that instinct, choosing stillness, waiting out the storm. But in that moment, stillness became exposure. Waiting became risk.

She didn't push him. Didn't yell. She just pivoted. Fast. Her shoulder clipped his as she passed, her pace already halfway to a sprint by the time he turned. The front door slammed behind her with a sound that didn't belong in a house that size. It hit the wall and bounced, rebounding shut with a hollow thud.

Jack stood there, hands still half-raised, like he wasn't sure what had just happened. He hadn't shouted. Hadn't grabbed her. Not really. But the look in her eyes when he stepped in her path had landed like a punch to the chest.

She hadn't looked afraid of the argument.

She had looked afraid of him.

It took a while for the realization to sink in. Even then, it didn't land cleanly. His mind insisted she was overreacting, that he hadn't meant to stop her from leaving, he had just wanted to finish the conversation. He wasn't trying to control her. He was trying to make sure she didn't shut him out again. He was trying to be present. Engaged. Committed.

But she didn't see it that way.

She saw a man in her space. A hand on her arm. A voice between her and the door.

This was the moment their dynamic changed. Not in a way either of them acknowledged out loud, but in a way they both felt.

Up until now, Lena had disengaged with confidence. Even in her silence, she'd had the upper hand, because silence was hers to control. Distance was her tool, not his punishment. She could withdraw and return on her terms. She could pause the tension without forfeiting her power.

But when Jack stepped in her path, she lost control over that, too. And in losing it, something in her snapped. Not with rage. Not with words. Just a sudden, undeniable certainty: she couldn't stay.

Not when disengagement wasn't respected. Not when walking away came with consequences.

Studies on emotional flooding in relationships describe this kind of escalation well. When the nervous system becomes overwhelmed, too much input, too little safety, the brain shuts down its capacity for rational processing. This is not simply being upset. It is panic without clarity. Fight-or-flight becomes the default response, even in emotionally charged, non-violent scenarios. People lash out or disappear not because they want to, but because their system cannot find a safe middle (Gottman & Levenson, 2000).

For Lena, the middle was where she'd lived for years. She had practiced disengagement like an art form, pausing conflict, shutting down before it peaked, distancing just enough to stay intact. But that kind of control only works when the other person respects the pause. When they understand the boundary for what it is. Jack never had.

To Jack, silence meant avoidance. He read her stepping back as a refusal to participate. As manipulation. As her way of getting the upper hand. He had never recognized it for what it was: her last attempt to keep things safe, for both of them.

What happened at the door wasn't Jack exploding. It wasn't even Jack losing control. It was Jack trying to reassert himself in the conversation. Trying to hold it together by stopping her from disappearing again.

But it didn't matter how calm his voice had been.

He had stepped between her and the door.

That image, the memory of that moment, stayed with Lena longer than any insult or argument ever could. She hadn't left the house because of what Jack said. She had left because of how small she felt when he decided he had the right to stop her.

That night marked the end of their old pattern.

It wasn't the worst fight they would have. It wasn't the last time Jack would push too hard or the last time Lena would shut down. But it was the moment that shifted the ground between them. Because for the first time, space wasn't something Lena had chosen. It was something she had to take back by force.

And Jack? He didn't chase her.

Not because he understood. Not because he regretted it. But because he didn't know what else to do.

It wasn't fear that kept him frozen. It was the dawning sense that he had crossed a line he couldn't name, one that might not look dramatic on the surface but felt unmistakable in her absence.

There was no apology. No explanation. No resolution. Just the echo of the door and the weight of what it meant.

Jack had wanted her to stay in the conversation.

She made sure he knew she wouldn't stay if she wasn't free to leave.

The Waiting Game: Jack's Attempt to Regain Control

Jack had always believed that time could fix things. That if you waited long enough, let the heat of an argument die down, let the dust settle, everything would return to normal. Time could smooth out the rough edges, dull whatever sharpness had made someone walk away in the first place.

That's what he told himself as he sat at the kitchen table, fingers drumming against the wood, foot bouncing restlessly against the floor.

Lena was gone.

The door had slammed. The car had started. The silence had stretched.

He wasn't chasing her. Not this time.

Not because he didn't want to. Not because he wasn't furious, or confused, or caught somewhere between knowing he had done something wrong and refusing to believe it was as bad as she had made it seem.

He wasn't chasing her because he didn't need to. She would be back.

She always came back.

Jack had learned that waiting worked just as well as chasing. In the beginning, he had pushed. Demanded she finish conversations she had already decided were over. Followed her into another room, pressed for an answer, refused to let her disengage without some kind of acknowledgment. It hadn't worked. If anything, it had made her retreat faster. But when he stopped following, when he sat in silence and let her leave, she always returned.

That's what he had figured out. That's what changed everything.

Lena needed space. Fine. He could give it to her. But space wasn't the same as freedom. If she wanted to leave, fine. But she would still come back on his terms.

Patience could be its own form of control.

Psychologists studying conflict resolution in couples note that disengagement can serve two different functions: self-regulation or power assertion (Overall & McNulty, 2017). For Lena, disengagement was about emotional regulation, controlling her exposure, managing her stress. For Jack, waiting became a tool to hold the power in the situation. By refusing to engage, by letting her leave and forcing her to come back, he controlled when they reconnected.

Lena thought she was reclaiming her autonomy when she walked away. She didn't realize she was giving him something in return. She was giving him proof.

Every time she left and returned without an apology, without an acknowledgment, without any indication that she had truly left him at all, she reinforced something in Jack's mind. She had walked away, but she had still come back. She had given him a reason to believe that it had never been as bad as she made it seem. If it had been, she wouldn't have returned. If it had been, she wouldn't be standing in the kitchen the next morning, pouring coffee like nothing had happened.

She made it easy to believe that the fight hadn't been as serious as it felt in the moment. That no matter how hard the door had slammed, no matter how long the silence had stretched, the end result was always the same.

She left.

He waited.

She came back.

And the waiting gave him a new kind of power.

Most people think control looks like confrontation. That it's loud, demanding, aggressive. That it looks like someone standing in front of a door, arms crossed, voice sharp with accusation.

But control can be quieter than that. More insidious. Control can look like patience.

Jack didn't need to chase her anymore. He had learned that if he waited, she would always come back to him. And when she did, the dynamic was already in his favor.

He wasn't the one who had walked out.

He wasn't the one who had refused to talk.

He wasn't the one who had turned his back.

And whether or not Lena realized it, that imbalance mattered.

She thought she was protecting herself when she left. But in doing so, she left Jack with something she never meant to give him, the ability to hold her return against her.

It was subtle at first. A look. A tone. A lingering silence when she walked back into the house and expected things to be fine. But sometimes, when she came back like nothing had happened, he'd let her know that he remembered. That she was the one who had left, and he was the one who had stayed. That she had walked out, and he had been the one waiting for her to come home.

Most of the time, he let it go.

But sometimes, when the silence stretched too long, when the fight sat too heavily between them, he reminded her that she owed him something for it. That she had been the one to abandon the conversation, to turn away when things got hard. That she had dictated the terms of their arguments one too many times, and it was his turn to demand something back.

And when she didn't give it, when she acted like she didn't understand, or like he was the one making too much of it, the fight started again.

Waiting was supposed to be about patience. About stepping back, about giving someone time to cool down, about letting things breathe. But in the wrong hands, waiting can become something else entirely. It can become a ledger. A scorecard. A weapon wrapped in restraint.

Jack didn't think of it that way.

But when he sat in the silence, convincing himself that patience would restore balance, that waiting her out was better than chasing her down, he wasn't thinking about resolution.

He was thinking about what she would owe him when she came back.

And she always came back.

Chapter Five

The Power Struggle – Who Wins When No One Backs Down?

The Anatomy of a Power Struggle

They say marriage is compromise, but Jack and Lena never got that memo. For them, compromise wasn't a noble aim, it was a trapdoor. The moment one of them relented, the other surged forward. Not maliciously. Not even consciously. But the dynamic was as predictable as it was exhausting: pull back, get chased. Push harder, get defied. There was no middle ground because middle ground meant someone had to yield, and neither one of them could stomach that.

A true power struggle isn't just a fight. It's not even about disagreement, at least not on the surface. You can argue over money, schedules, in-laws, toothpaste direction, but the actual terrain is something deeper, more primal. A power struggle is when the disagreement becomes a proxy war for identity. It's "You're not hearing me" weaponized into "You're trying to erase me." It's the sickening realization that if you give one more inch, you might disappear altogether.

For Jack, that fear of disappearing was visceral. If he couldn't shape the outcome, couldn't steer the course, then what was the point of being in the room? He wouldn't say it that way, of course. He'd say things like, "Why do you always push me away?" or "Why can't we just decide this together?" But underneath the words was a deeper panic: If I don't hold ground here, I cease to matter.

Dominance, for Jack, wasn't about getting his way. It was about staying in the game. It was a lifeline thrown into the chaos of emotional uncertainty. If he could hold the upper hand, even for a moment, he could breathe. He could believe, just a little, that he wouldn't be swallowed by the unpredictability of someone else's will. Because that's what scared him most: the idea that Lena might steer the ship without him, that she might not just act without consulting him, but feel without needing him.

Lena, of course, read it differently. Jack's need for input felt like interference. His urgency sounded like a demand. She wasn't resisting out of stubbornness, she was resisting because that's what she'd been trained to do. Her whole body carried the memory of decisions made for her, of moments when safety meant silence, of times when pushing back meant punishment. So when Jack leaned in, metaphorically or literally, her instinct was to pull away. Not to punish him. Not even to win. Just to breathe.

Backing down, for Lena, wasn't an option. Yielding meant more than losing a point, it meant inviting the erosion of her selfhood. She could almost feel the ground slipping away whenever she said yes to something she didn't want. Even something small. "Where do you want to eat?" "I don't care." "Okay, we'll go here then." And suddenly, that wasn't dinner, it was proof that her preferences didn't matter. That she'd handed over a piece of herself for the sake of peace.

Of course, Jack didn't want to erase her. That's the maddening part. He wanted Lena's full, unfiltered presence more than anything. But every time she held her line, he panicked. Because to him, autonomy felt like rejection. If Lena didn't need him to co-author the moment, what role did he even play? So he pushed harder, thinking maybe if he could just crack her resistance, she'd let him in again. And Lena, feeling the walls close in, pushed back even harder, until the entire moment collapsed under the weight of two people refusing to surrender the parts of themselves they couldn't afford to lose.

This wasn't just about control. It was about belonging. For Jack, having a say meant having a place. For Lena, keeping her space meant keeping herself intact. Neither of them were power-hungry. But both were terrified of being rendered irrelevant.

Power struggles have a way of camouflaging themselves. On the outside, it sounds like someone's overreacting. "Why are you so upset? It's not a big deal." "You're being ridiculous." "I was just asking a question." But the volume of the argument rarely matches the emotional stakes underneath it. "You never listen to me" isn't really about the dishes or the thermostat. It's "I am disappearing and no one is noticing." "Stop interrupting me" isn't just about conversational etiquette, it's "If I don't finish this sentence, I might lose my right to finish a thought at all."

The trap is mutual. Jack doesn't want to dominate, but he can't risk being invisible. Lena doesn't want to defy, but she can't afford to be overridden. Each one's defense looks like offense to the other. He sees her pulling away and thinks, She's shutting me out. She sees him advancing and thinks, He's trying to take over.

Even the light moments don't always stay light. A playful jab turns into a tug-of-war. A teasing remark becomes a dare. Jack jokes that she's always late; Lena narrows her eyes and returns fire. Neither one knows how they got from flirtation to fury, only that once they're in it, neither can back down. Because to back down would mean conceding not just the moment, but something sacred, some internal territory they've each fought too hard to protect.

There were times, rare, fleeting times, when they saw the trap coming. When Lena would pause, mid-escalation, and say, "Wait, what are we doing?" Or Jack would fall silent instead of pushing, clench his jaw, and walk away. But even those moments weren't victories. They were ceasefires. Temporary. Fragile. Because the battle wasn't about the present, it was about the past. About what had been taken, withheld, silenced, overridden.

When both people are fighting to preserve their right to exist on their own terms, any disagreement can become a standoff. And when survival strategies collide, even love can feel like war.

This is the anatomy of a power struggle: not a question of who's right, but of who's still standing. Not about logic, but about presence. About agency. About not letting someone else's need rewrite your own. And when both people are hell-bent on staying whole, there is no resolution, only resistance. Only tension masquerading as connection. Only two people bracing against each other, hoping that if they push just a little harder, the other will finally understand what it costs to yield.

The Beach Incident – Where It All Cracked Open

They had gone to the beach to reset. Not to fix anything, neither of them believed in easy fixes, but to breathe in a place where the air didn't already belong to their arguments. The ocean had always been good to them. Something about the way it roared louder than they ever could made their conflicts feel small for a while. Lena had picked the spot. Jack had packed the gear. It felt, briefly, like they were on the same team.

The water was cold but not cruel. Lena had waded in first, arms lifted above her head, toes curling into wet sand. Jack followed with the swagger of someone who couldn't stay serious for long. She smiled when he approached, just a small flicker of affection, the kind she didn't give away easily. Jack saw it and wanted more.

He lunged, caught her around the waist, and pulled her down with him into the surf. She shrieked, a startled, laughing sort of sound, and flailed, kicking at the salt and bubbles. He surfaced beside her, grinning, hair plastered to his forehead. "Got you," he said.

She slapped water at his chest. "You ass."

"Say that again," he teased, and dove toward her, arms reaching.

This time, she tried to dodge. He caught her anyway.

They wrestled in the shallows, wave after wave knocking them off balance. Lena was laughing, really laughing, until she wasn't. It happened fast. Jack's grip tightened around her ribs as he spun her sideways, water crashing over their shoulders. She yelped, not in delight this time, and tried to twist free, but he only whooped louder, tossing her backward like a rag doll into the next wave. A flash of something in her eyes. Her smile didn't just fade, it vanished. Her body stiffened beneath his hands, the way someone goes still before the break. She pushed at him, once, then twice. Not playfully.

"Jack," she said. "That's enough, stop."

But he didn't hear it the way she meant it. He was still caught in the rhythm of the moment, still trying to keep the energy alive. "Come on, don't be like that," he said, holding her tighter. "Lighten up."

Then, just as the next wave crested, he bent his knees and sprang upward, still gripping her waist, and together they went under, the salt and surge swallowing them whole. She pushed harder, but he mistook it for resistance, the kind that made him feel wanted, needed, engaged. He didn't realize it had become something else.

She went still. Not in surrender, but in freeze. It was the oldest reflex in her body. The one she hadn't chosen.

He held her underwater a second longer than her nervous system could tolerate. Not long enough to choke. Just long enough to panic.

She came up gasping, not for air, but for control. Her palms hit his chest, shoving him back with a force he hadn't expected.

"Stop!" she barked.

Jack blinked, confusion scrambling across his face. "I was just playing."

"No, you weren't. You weren't listening."

He stared at her, arms dripping, mouth parted like he wanted to argue but didn't know where to start. She was already walking away, water cascading off her as she moved toward shore.

It wasn't about the dunking. She'd been dunked a hundred times in her life. By friends, siblings, even Jack, before. But this time, she'd said no, and it hadn't mattered. That's what gutted her. That she had withdrawn consent mid-moment and he hadn't noticed. That she'd changed her mind, and his momentum had overruled her reality.

Her body wasn't afraid of water. It was afraid of being trapped. Pinned in a moment she couldn't exit. Her panic wasn't rational, it was cellular. A record scratch in her nervous system. And once it played, she couldn't unhear it.

Jack stood there in the shallows, watching her walk away. He didn't follow. Not right away. He let her go, physically, at least. Emotionally, he was still arguing with himself, still rearranging the memory into something less indicting. It was a joke. She was laughing. She overreacted.

Lena wrapped a towel around herself without speaking. Her hands shook a little, but she didn't make a scene. That would have given the moment too much oxygen. Jack eventually came up beside her, quietly. She didn't flinch. But she didn't lean in, either.

They stayed that way, side by side, wrapped in silence that wasn't quite peace.

He said something about grabbing food. She nodded. They moved through the next few hours like people who hadn't just hurt each other in a way neither could name. But they both knew. Something shifted in the water, and they had no words for it.

Later that night, she curled away from him in bed. Not angrily. Just protectively. Like her body was trying to redraw the boundaries that had been blurred. Jack reached for her, hesitant.

"Are you mad at me?"

She hesitated. "I'm not mad. I just... I didn't like it."

"I didn't mean anything by it," he said quickly. "You were laughing."

"I stopped," she said. Quietly. Almost too quietly.

He rolled onto his back and stared at the ceiling. "I didn't know."

And maybe he didn't. But that wasn't the point. The point was, she had known. And it hadn't mattered.

They didn't talk about it again.

It hadn't healed, but they didn't know how to stitch something invisible. The wound wasn't dramatic enough to call attention to itself. No screaming, no accusations. Just a shift. A quiet breakdown of trust in the space where "I was just playing" collided with "You didn't hear me."

That's how some of the worst damage happens. Not in crisis. In the spaces between. When no one names what went wrong, and both people pretend it didn't.

When Connection Requires Control

Jack wouldn't have called it control. Not consciously. To him, it was connection, staying in it, pushing through the silence, making sure the lines between them didn't go slack. He didn't need to win. He just needed to know the game was still on.

If Lena snapped at him, rolled her eyes, or pushed back with some barbed comment of her own, he could breathe. It meant she was still there. Still invested. Still reachable. It meant he hadn't lost her to that colder place, her detachment, her inner exile, the quiet that came after she decided there was no point in talking anymore.

What Jack couldn't handle was disengagement. Not just silence, but disappearance. The kind where Lena looked through him, not at him. The way her body could be in the same room while her mind curled away into some fortified corner he couldn't touch. That's when he panicked, not with fear, exactly, but with urgency. With a desperate need to make something happen.

So he'd say something to provoke her. Just enough to get a reaction. Sometimes he didn't even know he was doing it until it was too late. The words would be out, the temperature rising, and part of him would feel a flicker of relief. She was yelling now. Flushed. Furious. Present.

He could work with that.

Jack had learned long ago that resistance meant relevance. He came from a house where you weren't noticed unless you made noise. Where the only thing worse than being screamed at was being ignored. Where silence wasn't peace, it was exile.

So when Lena resisted him, part of him lit up. It gave him a role to play. A position to hold. She was engaging, and that meant he still mattered.

But when she didn't resist, when she just nodded or walked away, something darker crept in. It felt like abandonment, like being written out of the story mid-sentence. That was when the real escalation started. Not to punish her, but to reanimate the connection. To restart the emotional pulse between them. He needed the tension. Because without it, everything went flat.

He'd never say it that way, of course. He'd say she was being cold. That she was giving up too easily. That she didn't fight fair. But really, what he meant was: Don't go numb on me. Don't leave the room while still standing in it.

Jack didn't want to dominate. Not in the traditional sense. He didn't want Lena afraid of him, or obedient, or silenced. What he wanted was to feel that he could move her. That he had impact. That he could still shape the direction of the moment. Because if he couldn't, if she was immune to his words, untouched by his emotion, then who was he, exactly? What was the point of being there, loving her, fighting for anything at all?

Control, then, became his way of staying present. It's not that he craved power. He couldn't stand the alternative: irrelevance. He needed to feel that if he reached out, the world would ripple. That his voice could still shift the tone, even if just a little.

That's the seduction of the dynamic. In that tension, there was something electric, something that felt, to both of them, like aliveness. Like engagement. Like proof that what they had was still burning.

But it came at a cost.

Because the more Jack pressed, the more Lena defended. And the more she defended, the more Jack escalated, trying to break through. Each of them responding to the other's wound with their own, until what began as a bid for closeness turned into a reenactment of every buried trauma neither had fully named.

She felt trapped. He felt dismissed. She shut down. He shouted. And beneath it all was a mutual, aching truth: they didn't want to hurt each other. They just didn't know how to stop trying to prove they still mattered.

The real tragedy wasn't the fighting. It was that the fighting made them feel alive in ways that calm never did. It was that the fighting gave them a kind of intensity they couldn't find anywhere else. The silence was scarier than screaming. They both mistook the spark of resistance for the flame of connection.

They weren't wrong, entirely. There is something intimate about knowing exactly where your partner's boundary is, and choosing to press against it anyway. About being the person who can elicit the strongest reactions, even if those reactions burn. In a strange way, it made them feel known.

But the body doesn't care about intentions. It remembers only the pressure, the panic, the way safety drains out of a moment the second control replaces consent.

Jack didn't mean to override her. Lena didn't mean to disappear. But in their efforts to stay connected, they kept triggering the very responses that tore them further apart.

Because for Jack, connection required movement. Resistance. Impact.

And for Lena, safety required stillness. Autonomy. Escape.

They couldn't both have what they needed in the same moment, not without one of them surrendering something vital. And neither of them could afford to do that. Not yet.

Autonomy Isn't Rejection – But Jack Can't Hear That

Lena didn't fear closeness, not in the way people assumed. She could sit beside Jack for hours, knees brushing, silence wrapped around them like a shared blanket. She could tell him things that made her own voice tremble. Intimacy didn't scare her. What scared her was vanishing inside it.

She'd done that before. In other relationships. In her childhood. In moments when keeping the peace meant folding herself smaller, swallowing her preferences, smiling through discomfort. Every time she gave up a piece of herself to make someone else feel more secure, she chipped away at something essential. So now, even the suggestion that she should bend felt dangerous.

Jack didn't see it that way. To him, mutual decisions were the bedrock of commitment. "We're a team," he'd say. "We do things together." But for Lena, that kind of unity sometimes felt like pressure. Like a polite invasion. She didn't want to fight over dinner plans or weekend agendas, but when Jack kept asking for input, Where do you want to go? What do you want to do? Can we just agree on something?, she started to feel like she was being backed into a corner.

Her autonomy was oxygen. It wasn't about control or stubbornness, it was about breathing. When Jack insisted on locking into sync, she felt the walls close in. It wasn't his fault. He didn't mean to crowd her. But emotional safety for Lena meant having the space to move. To say no without consequence. To change her mind without being questioned. To need solitude without it becoming a referendum on the relationship.

But Jack couldn't hear "I need space" without translating it to "I don't want you."

He didn't just misinterpret Lena's autonomy, he feared it. Not in theory, but in the way a child fears silence after laughter. The quiet always felt like a bad sign. Like something had shifted and no one had said it out loud yet.

When Lena walked away to breathe, Jack felt her pulling the plug.

She'd head out to the porch or take a solo drive, trying to calm her system before things escalated. But in Jack's mind, every exit echoed with abandonment. She's shutting me out. She's done with me. She doesn't care. And once he was in that headspace, he couldn't let it go.

So he'd follow her. Not always physically. Sometimes it was through texts. Sometimes it was just pacing in the house, waiting for her to come back. Sometimes it was questions lobbed like grenades when she returned. "Are you just gonna run every time we disagree?" "Why can't we talk like adults?" "What is so hard about staying present?"

To him, presence meant staying in the room. Staying in the fight. Staying in the emotion, even if it was hot and messy and loud. Lena's version of presence was different. She needed to step outside the moment to feel safe inside it. Without the option to disengage, she couldn't stay grounded. And if she couldn't stay grounded, she couldn't stay at all.

Their definitions of safety diverged so completely, they didn't even realize they were chasing different things. Jack was trying to close the gap between them. Lena was trying to keep it wide enough to breathe. Both of them were terrified that if they didn't protect their version of safety, the relationship would eat them alive.

That's why the everyday arguments mattered so much. It was never just about the little things. Jack wanted her to come to a family dinner, she hesitated. He heard rejection. She felt pressure. He insisted. She shut down. By the end of the conversation, they were both blinking back tears for reasons neither could quite name.

It was the beach incident in miniature. A hundred versions of it, scattered across their weeks like emotional landmines. Lena would say no to something small, another show, another chore, another conversation she wasn't ready for. Jack would push because he couldn't understand why she'd say no in the first place. He wasn't demanding obedience. He was asking for reassurance. He was saying, Please still be here with me.

But Lena heard something else. She heard the sound of her boundaries cracking. She felt the weight of obligation pressing down on her chest. And so she disengaged.

Jack escalated.

That's how it always started. Not with rage or accusation, but with confusion. Hurt. A sense of loss so quiet it almost didn't register until it started to boil. Jack would feel it first in his tone, a little sharper, a little faster. Then in his chest, tight and hot. He'd press again. Why won't you just answer me? And by then, Lena would already be gone. Not literally. Just... gone.

That disappearance wrecked him. He needed to know he still existed in her world.

But for Lena, retreat was survival. Staying in the conversation once it crossed a certain threshold felt like agreeing to betray herself. She couldn't do it. Not anymore. Not for anyone.

They weren't speaking the same language. And worse, they didn't know how to translate. Jack needed affirmation. Lena needed air. Jack needed engagement. Lena needed escape. Jack needed to hear You matter. Lena needed to know I can say no and still be safe.

Neither of them was wrong. But every time they acted on their need, the other felt punished.

That's what made it so hard to untangle. The intention was never to hurt each other. The outcome just kept looking like harm.

When Nobody Backs Down, Nobody Wins

There's a point in every fight where the original issue becomes irrelevant. You forget whether you were arguing about whose turn it was to clean the kitchen, or whether one of you interrupted the other, or how loud the TV was playing. What remains is the standoff, the need to be right, to be seen, to not be the one who folds first.

For Jack and Lena, those moments weren't the exception. They were the rule. The escalation might look different each time, but it always ended in the same kind of exhausted silence. Sometimes after yelling. Sometimes after tears. Sometimes after that awful, aching quiet where neither of them said the one thing they actually meant: I'm scared you'll stop loving me if I don't win this one.

Stalemates like these don't just hurt in the moment. They accumulate. Like emotional debt. Every unresolved argument, every line neither was willing to cross or retreat from, chipped away at the trust between them. And over time, that debt added up. Little by little, they began to associate each other not just with love or longing, but with fatigue. With tension. With that sick feeling in your stomach when you know you're gearing up for another round.

The worst part? Even when one of them "won," nobody felt good about it.

When Jack pushed long enough and hard enough that Lena finally caved, when she said yes with her lips but no with her eyes, he didn't feel victorious. He felt empty. Hollow.

Like he'd gotten what he wanted, but lost something more important in the process.

And when Lena stood her ground, when she refused to be coerced or convinced, even at the cost of Jack's frustration, she didn't feel empowered. She felt isolated. Distant. Alone in her convictions.

There was no satisfaction. Only aftermath.

Jack would feel ashamed. Guilty. But also, somehow, justified. He'd tell himself he hadn't done anything wrong, not really. He hadn't screamed this time. He hadn't broken anything. But still, there was that feeling in his chest like he'd just wrecked the room and didn't know how to clean it up.

Lena didn't doubt what had happened. She was just tired, tired of flinching, tired of guarding herself, tired of pretending that Jack's good intentions made any real difference. A heavy, resentful anger stirred in her chest, louder than fear, colder than hurt.

Neither one trusted the resolution, because the resolution had cost too much. Jack had overstepped. Lena had withdrawn. One had spoken over the other. One had gone silent. And when they finally moved forward, it wasn't because anything had been resolved. It was because they were too tired to keep fighting.

That's the problem with chronic power struggles. Even when they quiet down, they don't actually end. They just go underground, waiting for the next trigger to pull them back into the same loop. And over time, those loops start to write the story of the relationship itself.

He doesn't listen.

She always leaves.

He can't get through to her.

He has to win.

These aren't just thoughts, they're narratives. Beliefs that calcify into truths, shaping the way each new interaction is interpreted. Jack might start a conversation gently, but Lena's already bracing for the push. Lena might ask for space, and Jack already hears the door closing behind her. They don't mean to script each other's behavior, but when the patterns keep repeating, it's hard not to.

And the deeper tragedy is this: neither of them is fighting to dominate. They're both fighting to be real to the other. To be held in their full, messy, contradictory selves without having to disappear. But when neither can back down, when surrender feels like annihilation, they end up proving their worst fears true.

Jack fears he doesn't matter. That if he loosens his grip, Lena will slip away and forget him.

Lena fears giving up the only thing she can still control: herself. That if she stops defending her autonomy, she'll vanish and Jack won't even notice she's gone.

So they stand their ground. Again and again. Until the ground becomes battlefield. And love becomes something they brace against, instead of something they rest in.

Reader Reflection Exercise

Power struggles are rarely about power. They're about identity, safety, and emotional survival.

Take ten minutes and answer the following questions as honestly as you can, no one else will read them.

1. When you argue with someone you love, what are you actually trying to protect? (Not what you're arguing about, but what you're afraid will happen if you give in.)

2. What does "losing" mean to you in a conflict? (Is it about being wrong? Being small? Being forgotten?)

3. Think of a time you "won" an argument but felt worse afterward. Why?

4. What does it feel like in your body when your autonomy is threatened?

5. How about when your relevance feels at risk?

6. What would it mean to "back down" without disappearing?

7. What would it mean for your partner to do the same?

Come back to these questions the next time you feel a standoff brewing. Let them soften the edges of your certainty. The goal isn't to stop fighting. The goal is to fight for each other, not just against.

Chapter Six

Breaking Points – The Moments That Define a Relationship

When does fear override love?

Not in theory, in motion. In breath. In muscle memory. In the split-second decision to hold on instead of let go, to restrain instead of release. When does the fear of losing control, or the fear of losing yourself, become stronger than reason, connection, or restraint?

This is that moment.

Not the worst fight they've ever had. Not the loudest. But the one where instinct took over. Jack's fear of abandonment met Lena's fear of captivity, and both of them crossed a line they couldn't uncross.

This is a story about the space just after survival. About what happens when the adrenaline fades, but the questions don't. When love still lingers, but trust can't get a foothold. When neither partner can pretend everything is okay, but neither one knows what comes next.

When Jack Crossed the Line

He didn't hit her.

That's the line Jack will cling to in the days to come. Like it's proof of something. Proof he didn't mean harm. Proof he's not his father. Proof there's still a line he won't cross.

But Lena's body doesn't care about the absence of a blow. It remembers the weight. The heat of his arms. The way her wrists folded in on themselves as she tried to push him off. It remembers the moment her breath stalled in her chest from the sheer realization: he's not letting go.

It starts like every other fight. Loud. Stupid. Off-course. She's already grabbed her bag by the time he cuts off her path to the door.

"You're not walking out in the middle of this," he says, voice sharp, too fast, the air around him jittering with the beginnings of panic.

"I'm not walking, I'm leaving," she snaps, stepping right. He blocks again.

"You always run when it gets hard."

"Jack, move."

She's not shouting. Not yet. But there's an edge now, a slice of warning in her voice. That tone she uses when her hands start to shake and her chest gets tight and her brain splits in half: one side still fighting, the other already calculating exit routes.

"Every single time," Jack growls, closer now. "You throw a match and walk away. Like I'm just supposed to stand here burning."

His breath is hot, wild. Lena steps back.

This is not about the thing they were fighting about. She can't even remember what it was. Dishes, probably. Or whether he meant something by the way he looked at her earlier. Or whether she sighed too hard when he made that joke.

It's never the thing. It's always the feeling under the thing. The thrum of a power struggle that never sleeps.

"You don't get to disappear!" Jack barks. "Not this time!"

And then it happens.

He reaches for her arm. She jerks back. He grabs harder.

"Let go!"

"No, you're not leaving me like this!" He pulls her to him, arms wrapping around her waist.

Then Lena yells. She doesn't even know what she's saying, just that it's loud, sharp, breaking through the tension with a scream meant to reset the moment. Like maybe if she shouts loud enough, he'll snap out of it. Like maybe her panic can substitute for reason.

But Jack doesn't let go.

She fights him, twisting, trying to get her arms free from his hold. He grips tighter. She kicks, but his legs are locked in place. They fall to the floor, his arms caging her.

"Jack, stop! Stop!"

He doesn't hear her. Or maybe he does, but her voice just makes him angrier. Sharp, high, defiant. Like always. Like she thinks she gets to decide when this ends.

He's not thinking. He's reacting. Fast. Brutal. Like the part of his brain built for mercy just shut off.

She's fighting him, but he holds tighter.

"Goddammit, stop!" he snaps. "Just stop!"

That's what comes out.

Not fear. Not longing. Not even anger that makes sense. Just the guttural, wounded demand of someone whose world is slipping through his fists and would rather break it than watch it leave.

Lena goes still.

This is the moment.

Not because she's calm. She's not. But because she understands, viscerally, that nothing she says will reach him. This isn't Jack anymore. Not the Jack who teases her for hoarding books or kisses her forehead in the morning as she sleeps. This is the version of him that comes out when he's losing control, and needs to take it back by force.

Not fists. Not bruises. Just weight. Just refusal.

She can't breathe.

His face is so close she can feel his breath. His arm is across her chest and his weight bearing down on her. Her legs are pinned. She thrashes, but nothing moves.

Her lungs seize. She starts to panic. This is danger. She stops. She goes still.

Not surrender, strategy. Her body shuts down to survive.

Jack doesn't notice at first. His breath is ragged. He's still locked in.

Then, the fight is over. Jack releases his grip, and rises back to his feet.

Lena is numb. She slowly rises to her feet, and walks away from that spot, and Jack.

Jack watched her move, dazed, like he's just woken up from a trance.

"Lena..."

But she's in protection-mode. She moves slowly and carefully, picking up fallen trinkets and replacing them, tidying up the aftermath of clutter in the room.

He's reaching for her again, not to restrain, this time, but to explain. To apologize. To fix it.

She looks at him, her eyes empty.

Jack knew she had shut down, it was over. He went outside on the back porch to give Lena some space.

Out the door. Keys, coat, purse.

Her breath rips out in gasps as she starts the car and slams it into gear. She doesn't know where she's going. Only that she's going away.

Behind her, she hears his voice, faint, maybe calling her name. Maybe pleading.

But it doesn't matter.

Because as she disappears into the night, Lena's last clear thought slices through the blur:

He doesn't know what he just did. But I do.

The Fallout

She made it out.

That should have been the hard part. The fight, the weight of him, the house disappearing in her rearview mirror.

But the hard part is what comes after.

Not the silence. She's used to that. Grew up in it. Learned how to breathe through it without making a sound.

The hard part is how functional she feels. No collapse. No sobbing. No dramatic reckoning. Just sharp, alert stillness. Like her body knows she's not done yet.

She moves on autopilot. Bag by the door. Keys within reach. Checks the window locks without thinking. Counts outlets. Shadows. Escape points. She doesn't sit long, doesn't unpack. Doesn't get comfortable. Comfort isn't the point.

She doesn't cry. Not that night. Not the next morning either. What would be the use? Crying takes space. Crying is indulgent. She's not in mourning, she's in assessment. And feeling too much right now would slow her down.

It's not that she's numb. She's not. She feels plenty. But it's layered beneath muscle and instinct. Ready to strike if needed. She isn't unraveling. She's cataloging. Every detail. Every reaction. Every variable in the room.

She doesn't try to sleep. She positions herself with her back to the wall, one foot on the floor, eyes open long after the lights go out.

This isn't panic.

This is the freeze.

The kind you learn when resistance won't save you, but staying alert might.

Lena knows it well. Knew it by age five. When someone bigger than you decides your voice is inconvenient, your fear a burden, your body a thing to be overruled "for your own good", this is what you learn to do. You go still. You go quiet. You don't scream, because no one will come. You don't fight, because that makes it worse. You wait. And when it's over, you don't feel anything, because the body shuts the door and bolts it.

What happened with Jack wasn't a repeat. It was a rhyme. Her wrists pressed down, his voice echoing in her ears, all layered over the memory of another man's rules, another house where "discipline" meant obedience and silence was a virtue.

Jack didn't hit her.

Her nervous system doesn't care about nuance. It doesn't weigh motive or context. It doesn't ask what he meant. It only knows: threat. Trapped. Crushing weight. Constricted breathing. No way to break free.

The details keep flashing back, his voice, the pressure, the moment her body gave up the fight so her brain could survive it.

She doesn't need to unravel the why. She's lived through worse with better intentions.

What matters is he didn't stop.

He felt her struggling. Heard her panic. And he kept going. That's the part that sticks. Because if he believed he had the right to hold her down, if he thought that was justified, then he's dangerous.

Not only when he's angry. When he wants control. When he *needs* control.

And now she knows that. In her bones.

It doesn't make her hate him, although she really doesn't like him right now.

It just means she'll never assume she's safe again.

Lena's strength doesn't come from optimism. It comes from grit. From a childhood where safety was performance, and protection came with conditions. She learned to read the room before it exploded. Learned when to stay silent. When to disappear.

She thought she'd outgrown all that. That the version of her who walks away now isn't the same girl who curled up in her closet to wait out the storm.

But when Jack pressed his body over hers, when her mind filled with that hot, tight fear, she knew: her body hadn't forgotten a thing.

This is the part no one sees. Not even Jack. Especially not Jack.

He'll talk about the fight, rationalize *if only she hadn't been screaming*. Maybe apologize. Maybe say he "lost it," that he didn't know what he was doing. He'll frame it as a moment. A mistake. *Her* mistake.

But Lena's body is living the sequel. Quietly. Relentlessly.

She hesitates at doorways. Her ears track noise she doesn't consciously hear. Every vibration in her pocket gets clocked as potential threat. *Is it him?*

And it's not because she's weak. It's because she's wired for survival. She made it out.

But some part of her is still on that floor. Pinned. Breath tight. Waiting for the pressure to shift. Waiting for the danger to pass.

She wants to believe he'll feel it, the weight of what he did. Not just the act. But the impact.

She wants that. But she knows better.

She knows he didn't recognize what her silence meant. He didn't stop because he understood. Because the truth is, she knows he mistook it for surrender.

And now, in the dull hush of a borrowed guest room with borrowed sheets, she finally lets the question rise, the one she hasn't dared to ask until now.

"Why would I ever go back?"

Jack's Version

Jack doesn't sleep. Not really. He lies still, stares at the ceiling, listens to the hum of a fridge that hasn't made a sound in hours.

The house feels hollow without her. Not quiet, vacant. Like someone hit mute on everything that made it home.

He keeps replaying the fight. Not all of it, just certain parts. Her voice, sharp with accusation. Her eyes, full of exit. The moment she grabbed her bag like that was it. Like he didn't even matter. Like the whole thing wasn't worth another word.

And then, her gone. The car engine. Silence.

He clenches his jaw tight, his fingers fidget under the blanket. He doesn't want to remember the part where he lost it. But it's in there. Just flickers. Her struggling. The heat between them, not passion, panic. His hands holding her down. Her voice breaking on his name.

But it didn't mean what she thinks it did.

He didn't hurt her.

He just... couldn't let her leave like that.

Not again. Not in the middle of things. Not when everything was unraveling and she refused to even try to understand. It's always the same, one tough conversation and she's grabbing her keys. She knows what that does to him. She knows. And she does it anyway.

He didn't plan to pin her down like that. He didn't even realize what he was doing until she went quiet. And by then, it was too late. But even that feels wrong. Like too late implies intent. He didn't mean for it to go there. It just... did.

Because she was out of control. Not crying. Not calm. Just saying things to provoke him. Tearing into him, screaming at him like she wanted him to snap. And what was he supposed to do? Let her leave thinking she was right? Let her twist it all up in her head like she always does?

He told her to stop. He begged her to be reasonable. She was the one who escalated. He just reacted.

Jack leans forward, elbows on knees, face in his hands. The shame is there, low and slow, crawling through his gut like something alive, but he keeps trying to tamp it down. Press it into something smaller. Something he can manage.

He didn't hit her.

That matters.

He didn't break anything. Didn't call her names. Didn't threaten her.

So why does it feel like he crossed some kind of line?

He shakes his head. This is the part where the two versions of himself start to argue.

One side whispers: You held her down. You didn't let go. You watched her panic and kept going.

The other side bites back: She freaked out. She always does. You were just trying to stop her from screaming at you.

It's not denial. It's survival.

Because if Jack lets himself believe he really hurt her, not just scared her, not just lost control, but hurt her, what does that make him?

His father?

The question curls in his chest like smoke.

No. No, that's not fair. He's not that man. He doesn't rage for fun. Doesn't throw punches. Doesn't treat people like they're disposable.

He loves Lena.

He was trying to hold on to her, not break her.

But love isn't what she saw in that moment. He knows that. Somewhere, deep under all his justifications, he knows.

And yet the words keep forming anyway:

"She overreacted." "She was in my face, screaming at me." "She always threatens to leave."

"I just snapped."

The more he says them, to himself, silently, the more real they feel. As if repetition can turn narrative into truth.

He wishes she'd call. Or text. Even just to curse him out. At least then he'd know she was still in it.

Instead, nothing.

He runs his hands through his hair. Opens his mouth like he might speak, then closes it again. There's no one here to hear him. No one to argue with but himself.

And he's losing.

He doesn't want her to think he's a monster. He wants her to stop acting like he did it on purpose. Like she wasn't screaming at him. Like she didn't push him first. He wants her to remember how out of control she was. How she baited him, cornered him, blew everything out of proportion.

It's not his fault. He just... snapped.

He wants her to let it go. To stop acting like it meant something it didn't. He wasn't trying to hurt her. He was trying to stop her from acting crazy, again.

She pushed. She provoked. She blew it up like she always does, then ran out the door and made him the bad guy.

If she comes back, it proves it wasn't what she's making it out to be.

If she comes back, it means she knows he didn't mean anything by it. That it was a fight. That she overreacted.

She knows he'd never hurt her. He loves her. He'd do anything for her. And she loves him.

That's why she'll come back.

That's what he tells himself, because the only thing worse than what he did is having to admit it might've actually meant something.

Why She Came Back

She didn't forgive him, she just wasn't done.

That's the part even she struggles to explain, to herself, to the friend who offered her a couch, to the version of herself that packed a bag and swore she wouldn't go back.

It would be easier if it were forgiveness. Cleaner. At least then she could point to some act of redemption, some line he crossed back over to earn her return. But it wasn't that. It was something murkier. Something closer to unfinished business. Something closer to survival logic dressed up as choice.

Because leaving didn't feel like freedom. It felt like suspension. Like the scene cut to black before the story finished writing itself.

Lena spent eight days away. Not because she was unsure. But because she needed to be certain about what came next. She expected no apology, nor would she entertain one at this point. She needed a read; to see what kind of man he was going to be now, in the aftermath.

And the longer she stayed away, the more defined things became. If she returned, it would be on new terms. The kind that didn't require discussion. What happened that night would never happen again. Not if she had any control over it. That was the line. The non-negotiable.

She wasn't going back because she doubted herself. She was going back to make sure he understood exactly what crossing a non-negotiable boundary would cost *him*.

Jack wasn't stupid. He'd know what her return meant. It wasn't forgiveness, it was a warning shot.

He needed to see the line he crossed. He needed to know: you don't get to do that and still keep me.

She wasn't looking for closure. She was looking for proof. That he got it. That he wouldn't do it again. That she didn't have to burn the house down to make him hear her. Because Jack had crossed a line, yes. But lines don't erase history. They just change the terms going forward.

What she didn't know, what she still hadn't seen, was what came after. After the weight of what he'd done, and the length of her absence finally caught up with him.

That's what pulled her back. Not hope. Inquiry.

She didn't text first. She just showed up, keys in hand, jaw set, one foot in the doorway and the other already braced for flight. Jack was sitting on the couch, staring blankly at a muted TV, and when he looked up, he didn't say anything. Just stood. Just blinked.

Neither of them moved.

She set her bag down slowly. Not in the bedroom. In the hall. Close to the door.

His voice, when it came, was small. "You okay?"

She didn't answer that. Just nodded once and walked past him into the kitchen. Opened the fridge. Closed it again.

Jack hovered, unsure. "I wasn't sure you'd..."

She looked at him then. Hard. Unreadable. He didn't finish the sentence.

They didn't talk about it that night. Not directly. Lena asked if the mail came. Jack said yeah. She asked if he'd eaten. He said he wasn't hungry.

He didn't apologize.

Not yet.

And she didn't ask for one.

Not yet.

She needed to see first.

Because apologies were his specialty. He could confess anything in the aftermath. Could weep at the altar of his own remorse and promise her the world if it meant resetting the board.

But she didn't need a performance. She needed evidence.

So she watched.

She paid attention to the way he moved when she entered a room. The way his voice softened or didn't. The way he touched her, or chose not to. She noticed the space he gave her. The distance he kept.

She tested small things. Disagreements. Tone. Timing. She needed to know if he could regulate himself now that he'd seen what lived on the other side of control. She needed to know if the restraint that had once flattened her would now be turned inward, toward himself.

Jack seemed careful. Too careful, maybe. Like he was walking on glass, trying not to breathe too hard. But Lena didn't mind that part. It wasn't peace. But it was pressure taken off the boil.

Still, she didn't relax. She didn't settle. She kept her bag near the door. She kept her voice even. And when Jack tried to lean in, just a little, just to see if she'd soften, she shifted back. Not cold. Just... aware.

He didn't ask why she'd come back. She didn't tell him.

But late that night, while he slept on the far edge of the bed and she stared up at the ceiling tracing the cracks in the plaster, the thought finally settled:

She wasn't here because she believed him. She was here because she needed to see what he'd do next.

That was the difference between hope and vigilance. Between forgiveness and unfinished reckoning.

She wasn't waiting for him to earn her back. She wasn't offering herself up for another try. She was watching. Measuring. Giving him one inch, not of her trust, but of her attention.

Part of her needed to believe that what happened mattered. That he felt the shift. That he understood, on some level, how close he came to losing her for good. And maybe, just maybe, what he did next would tell her whether he saw her as someone worthy of real respect, or just a storm he planned to wait out.

Because this time, she wouldn't argue. She wouldn't explain why it was wrong, or how it hurt, or what it brought back. She wouldn't plead for insight or accountability. That was her old pattern.

This time, she'd let the silence do the talking.

Let him wrestle with it.

Let him choose.

Because if he didn't, if he defaulted to shame or blame or revision, then she'd have her answer.

And if he didn't?

If he did the one thing he never could before, if he held himself accountable without her forcing it?

Then maybe, maybe, there was still a chapter left to write.

But she wasn't writing it for him.

She was waiting to see if he'd learned to hold a pen without turning it into a weapon.

The Real Breaking Point

The moment Jack held Lena down wasn't the end.

It felt like it at the time. Like something irreversible had happened. Like a truth had been exposed and would now reshape the rest of the story. And maybe it did. But what Lena learns in the days that follow is this: the real damage wasn't done in that moment. It was done in the stillness that followed. In the way the world kept turning like nothing had happened. In the way Jack made eggs the next morning after her return, quieter than usual but not shaken. In the way he kept talking around it like maybe if they both pretended hard enough, it would fade into the wallpaper with all the other messy things they never really fixed.

The incident itself was horrifying, but what haunts her is how normal it seemed.

Not because it wasn't serious, but because it didn't leave a mark you could point to. No bruises. No threats. She ran, and he let her. And when she came back, he greeted her like she was just late getting home from work.

That's the part she can't shake. The longer she sits with it, the more she understands: the breaking point wasn't that night. It was after.

The silence. The shame. The way she kept measuring his behavior like it could answer a question he refused to ask. The way he tiptoed around her like a man trying to fix something without admitting he broke it. The way she kept hoping he'd bring it up, say I know what I did, so she wouldn't have to.

Jack's journey back to himself, if there is one, starts here. Not with the act, but with what he chooses to do in the shadow of it. Whether he names it. Whether he owns it. Whether he learns how to sit with the weight of what he did without folding into shame or fleeing into blame.

But Lena's recovery begins here too.

Because this time, she's not waiting for him to call it what it was. She already knows. She felt it in her skin. She carries it in the way she watches him now, not with fear, but with a kind of wary distance. A new awareness of how easily she can be overpowered when someone she loves decides that a challenge is a fight he has to win.

Coming back was the beginning of a countdown.

Make a Difference with Your Review

Help Someone Just Like You Find the Right Book

> "To give without expecting anything in return, that's real power."
>
> unknown

If this book meant something to you, if it made you think, cry, reflect, or breathe a little deeper, would you consider helping someone else find it?

Most people choose what to read based on what others say. Your words could help someone who's hurting, searching, or stuck in the same kind of fight you've been through.

This book was written for people in messy, real relationships, where love and struggle live side by side. Where walking away is tempting, but fighting for love still matters.

Leaving a review takes less than a minute, costs nothing, and might help:

...one more person realize they're not crazy.
...one more partner put the pieces together.
...one more woman feel seen.
...one more man take a hard look at himself.
...one more relationship reach a turning point.

Want to help someone just like you?

Just visit the link or scan the code:
https://www.amazon.com/review/review-your-purchases/?asin=B0F6MJK1RY

If you've ever felt alone in the fight for love, you know how much it matters to be understood. Thank you, truly, for helping someone else feel that too.

With gratitude,
Renae C. Linde

PART III: BREAKING PATTERNS, BUILDING STRENGTH

Focus on disruption and reckoning. The moment after the fire, where accountability, repair, and truth-telling either happen or don't.

Chapter Seven

Emotional Triggers and the Science of Reactivity

Where Remorse Meets Reality and Still Falls Short

Not every wound is loud. Some arrive quietly, disguised as familiar words, a familiar look, a familiar silence. And some couples, like Jack and Lena, don't just survive these moments. They cycle through them. Over and over again.

This chapter isn't about communication tips. It's about what happens before the words. The instant when a partner's face changes and something ancient wakes up in your chest. The breath you don't take. The reaction that feels less like a decision and more like gravity.

Jack's explosive remorse feels genuine, but remorse, without change, becomes its own kind of trap. Lena, once comforted by his apologies, now sees them as the start of another loop. Together, they must reckon with the patterns they mistake for passion, the shame they confuse with progress, and the distance that grows each time repair is promised but not delivered.

Because real change doesn't begin with a better apology. It begins with learning to stop the spiral before it starts.

And for Jack and Lena, that may be the hardest thing they've ever had to do.

The Shame That Follows the Storm

Jack always knows the moment it's over, not when the fight stops, but when he stops fighting. There's a gap, just seconds long, when the heat drains from his body and something cold settles in. Not numb, just still. His jaw tightens, then releases. His hands open and close, slow and aimless, like his body's running some background process he can't shut off. He doesn't move, doesn't speak. The words he just said loop in his mind, sharp, final, echoing louder in the silence than they ever did out loud.

He can't take them back, but oh, he wants to.

That moment is when the shame begins. And once it starts, it doesn't stop.

What follows is as predictable as the explosion itself. Jack drops from rage into remorse like a man free-falling through his own conscience. It isn't performative or strategic. In those post-crisis minutes, he is wrecked, physically and emotionally. His mind runs back over the last ten minutes like a crime scene, searching for where it all slipped beyond his control. And it did slip. He knows that. What he doesn't always admit, what he can't always admit, is that it wasn't the first time. And if he doesn't do something different, it won't be the last.

Physiologically, the aftermath of anger is its own kind of crash. In the heat of escalation, Jack's body floods with adrenaline, his heart rate spikes, his blood vessels constrict, his pupils dilate, his muscles tense. He is no longer reasoning, he is reacting. His amygdala is in charge, and the rest of his brain has been told to shut up and sit down (Siegel, 2012). Once the threat passes, once Lena has stopped talking or left the room or started crying, whatever finally shifts the dynamic, his body begins its descent. Cortisol follows the adrenaline, and soon after, comes the depletion. The crash is not symbolic. It is chemical. It feels like hitting the ground after a long, manic sprint: legs aching, lungs on fire, heart drowning in its own rhythm.

In those moments, Jack can barely speak. The anger's gone, but its residue remains, heavier, more suffocating than the fury itself. He walks into the next room, or sinks to the floor where he stood, sometimes with his head in his hands, sometimes just staring into space like he's hoping time will crawl back and undo itself. He wants to reach for Lena, to say something, but he's not sure what would help. Or worse, he's sure nothing will.

This is when the inner monologue starts. I didn't mean to. I didn't want this. I was pushed. I hate that I did this. I hate that I keep doing this. It's a familiar script, not because it isn't true, but because it is, over and over again. Jack has repeated this descent so many times he knows its landmarks. The disbelief. The regret. The loathing. The silent plea for a sign that Lena still sees something in him worth staying for.

And once upon a time, she did.

There was a time when Lena didn't leave right away. She'd linger just long enough to see if Jack meant what he said. Not with comfort, never that, but with presence. She'd sit on the far end of the bed, arms crossed, eyes wary. Sometimes she stayed the night. Sometimes she didn't. But when she did, it wasn't forgiveness. To Jack, it felt like it. He latched onto it like a drowning man finds driftwood: desperate, grateful, relieved. He mistook her stillness for softness, her silence for reconciliation. He never questioned whether she was okay. Her staying meant he had been forgiven. And to him, that meant the bond held.

But something has changed. Lately, Lena's silence is no longer tender. It is distance. It doesn't offer comfort, it withdraws it. She doesn't sit with him anymore. She doesn't reach for him. Sometimes she doesn't even speak. And Jack feels it like a second punishment, harsher than the first. The worst part? He still thinks she's wrong.

Wrong for pushing. For walking away. For escalating. If she hadn't said what she did, or looked at him like that, or refused to answer, then maybe he wouldn't have lost it. Maybe they wouldn't be here again. He doesn't say it out loud, but it's there. A quiet mutiny in his chest, rewriting the story before it cools.

And yet, by the time the shame finally breaks through, Jack's already rewritten the narrative. Not maliciously. Just... self-protectively. She pushed. He reacted. It's over now. Still, something lingers. A weight. A hum beneath the surface that builds until he can't ignore it.

That's when he reaches for Lena.

Not to ask how she's doing, but to ease whatever's left inside him. He wants her closeness to settle the unrest. Her presence to mean we're fine. He doesn't frame it as absolution. But that's what it is. A quiet plea for relief that sounds like reconciliation.

But comfort, when it comes too easily, doesn't heal anything.

It just resets the timer.

Jack tells himself that guilt counts for something. That feeling bad, even if it comes late, makes him different than the kind of man who doesn't care. And maybe it does. He's not indifferent. But guilt without action isn't redemption. It's inertia.

And Lena no longer trusts it.

She's been drawn in by the weight of his remorse before. Mistook his discomfort for accountability. It took her years to see it clearly: his self-loathing didn't make her safer. It made her invisible. Because when he finally unraveled, it wasn't her pain on the table, it was his. And he expected her to meet it with compassion, while hers still lay raw and unattended.

There's no solace in watching someone spiral when you're still bleeding from the last impact.

Now, she stays quiet. Sometimes she leaves the room. Sometimes the house. Sometimes she just disappears into herself, eyes glassy, body distant, her silence cutting deeper than any accusation ever could. And Jack, left alone in the wreckage, doesn't know how to read it. He doesn't think she's withholding forgiveness. She stayed, so in his mind, it's over. If she's still distant, that's on her. He's moved on.

She's just tired.

Tired of doing the emotional labor for two people. Tired of patching wounds that never get time to close before they're torn open again. Tired of trying to stay close to a man who doesn't see what he's broken, or that anything's broken at all.

Jack's not cruel. But in the aftermath of his worst moments, he shifts quickly. Gets quiet. Moves on. He doesn't sit in it, not yet. There's too much to do, too much daylight left. The shame gets buried so he can function. And by the time it finally surfaces, hours or even days later, it's reframed to make sense to him.

He doesn't reach for her with understanding. He reaches with discomfort. With the need to clear the weight, not carry it.

But Lena doesn't need his shame. She needs his change.

She needs him to sit in that wreckage without making her responsible for clearing it. To speak, not just of how sorry he is, but of what he's going to do differently. She needs his remorse to be a launch point, not a lullaby. A beginning, not a ritual.

But Jack doesn't know how to do that. Not yet.

And so the cycle begins again. The crash, the avoidance, the return. And her silence, growing heavier with every repetition. Not because she wants to punish him. But because she can't keep surviving the same earthquake, hoping this time the walls will hold.

The Apology Loop – Why Remorse Isn't Redemption

There was a time when Lena would have clung to an apology like it meant something. Back then, hearing Jack say the words, I'm sorry. I hate what I did. I never want to hurt you again, was enough to soften the edge of what had just happened. She took it as a signal that he saw her pain. That he was still reachable. That maybe he could change.

Now, she's not so sure.

Apologies don't carry the same currency anymore. They've become familiar. Practiced. Almost rehearsed in their rhythm. Jack's apologies still hit all the right beats, regret, self-loathing, even acknowledgment, but they no longer sound like revelation. They sound like routine. And Lena, once comforted by that sincerity, now hears something else: a loop.

Not a resolution. Not a repair. Just the next turn of a circle she's already walked too many times.

There's a difference, she's learning, between regret and responsibility. One says, I feel bad. The other says, I need to change. Jack doesn't sit in regret, he manages it. Buries it until it's quiet enough to name. And when he finally does speak, it's calculated. A measured tone, a careful choice of words. Enough to suggest he's sorry. Enough to move on. And for a while, Lena took that as progress. Not because it comforted her, but because it kept the peace. But there's a hollow echo in it now. Because feeling bad has never been the issue. Jack always feels bad. The question is, what does he do with that feeling?

That's where things start to fall apart.

He doesn't plan his outbursts. Lena knows that. He doesn't plot ways to hurt her or manipulate her into submission. What happens between them, what erupts between them, is reactive. Explosive. And that's exactly the problem.

Jack sees his volatility as proof that he's not a bad man. Because if he didn't mean to do it, then maybe it doesn't count in the same way. Maybe it's just something that happened in a moment of overwhelm. Something out of his hands. You cornered me. I snapped. He doesn't say these things to avoid guilt, he says them because that's how it feels. In the moment, his mind narrows to a single focus: survival. He's no longer solving conflict. He's fighting for psychic air. And when the world narrows like that, so does responsibility.

But this is where it gets dangerous.

Because the more Jack leans on the narrative of reaction, the more he frames himself as a man without control over his own actions. And while that may offer some emotional distance from the shame, it does something far more damaging to Lena: it traps her.

If his actions are uncontrollable, then her safety depends entirely on how well she manages the escalation. It puts the burden back on her shoulders. Don't push too hard. Don't say the wrong thing. Don't walk away too quickly or look too cold or get too quiet. She becomes not just his partner, but his regulator. And once that happens, the dynamic is no longer mutual. It's conditional. It's survival-based.

Lena has started to feel that in her bones.

And so, she's stopped listening to Jack's apologies for their content. She listens for the space between the words. For the signs that anything has actually changed. Because remorse, by itself, is cheap. Painful, yes. Genuine, sure. But cheap, nonetheless, when it costs nothing and changes nothing.

She learned that the hard way.

Not too long after her return, there was a night when Jack came closer than ever to breaking through. The fight had been bad. Not violent, but intense. Words thrown like knives, each of them cutting deeper than they meant to. Jack had shouted something, she doesn't even remember what, and then, just as suddenly, he was quiet. He slumped against the wall like someone had turned off his power. Sat on the floor, head in his hands. His voice cracked when he finally spoke. I can't believe I said that. I hate myself right now. You didn't deserve that. I'm so sorry. I don't know why I do this.

And in that moment, Lena believed him. Not because the words were perfect, but because the ache in his voice felt real. It disarmed her. She sat beside him. They didn't talk much, but she stayed. They slept in the same bed that night, silent, close, suspended in that fragile calm that always follows chaos.

But the next time they fought, it happened again. Different trigger, same pattern. Jack lashed out. The apology came fast, like it had already been waiting backstage. And this time, Lena didn't sit with him. She went to bed alone.

That was the night she realized she'd been looking for the wrong signal. Words are easy. They're the first thing people learn to use when they want to keep someone close. But change? Change doesn't come out of your mouth. It shows up in the choices you make the next time you want to burn the house down.

Lena doesn't believe in perfect control. She knows what trauma can do to a nervous system. She knows what it's like to shut down before she even realizes she's afraid. To go still, go silent, go somewhere else in her mind, just long enough to survive the moment. The body always moves faster than the brain when danger feels familiar. She knows Jack's rage isn't about her. But it still hits her. And that means it's his to deal with. Whether it's planned or not. Whether it's instinct or not. Whether it feels automatic or not. Because impact doesn't care about intent. Not in the moment. Not after the fifth apology in as many weeks.

What Jack still struggles to understand is that remorse, while necessary, is not redemptive. It can't undo what's been done. It doesn't restore the parts of Lena that brace every time his voice sharpens. It doesn't change the way she tracks his mood across the room. Doesn't quiet the part of her that watches for the next shift. It doesn't stop her from pulling back at night, because staying close feels too much like surrender.

Apologies can't rebuild trust. Only different behavior can do that.

Lena's stopped hoping for poetic apologies. She's listening for the silence before the storm, Will he catch himself this time? Will he slow down? Will he walk away instead of charging forward? That's what matters now. Not what he says, but what he does. Not how much he hates what he did, but how far he'll go to prevent it from happening again.

Jack doesn't realize yet that his apologies, sincere as they may be, are starting to sound like closure to him, and like warning signs to her.

Because for Lena, a man on his knees isn't a promise. It's a pattern.

And she's learned how to read it.

She still remembers how he looked at her after that fight, eyes softened just enough to register regret. He had a controlled stillness about him, like he was showing her just enough vulnerability to close the distance. And he said the things she used to need to hear: That will never happen again. I love you. You don't know how much I love you.

She didn't respond.

He waited.

And when she didn't move, his voice dropped, calmer, gentler, like proximity alone might count as progress. She almost reached for him. Almost let the words be enough.

Almost forgot what came before.
Two weeks later, they fought again.
Same trigger. Different night.
No soft words this time.
He shouted.
He said things even worse than before.

And when it was over, when the silence fell and the shame set in, he reached for the same script. Word for word. Like nothing had happened in between. Like nothing had been learned. Like Lena hadn't sat there, just weeks earlier, telling herself maybe this time it will be different.

That was the moment it clicked.

Not that he didn't mean what he said. But that meaning it wasn't enough.

Because if remorse always leads back to the same apology, and never to new behavior, it isn't repair.

It's rehearsal.

The Psychology of the Trigger – How the Past Hijacks the Present

The worst fights between Jack and Lena don't start with shouting. They start with something quieter. A shift in posture. A word left unanswered. A question repeated one too many times. A look that lingers just a little too long. By the time either of them realizes they've crossed into dangerous territory, their bodies have already decided for them. And it's not about logic. It's not even about each other.

It's about memory. Stored, silent, unfinished.

When the nervous system registers a threat, especially one that mirrors old pain, it doesn't wait for context. The brain hands over control to the amygdala, the part that responds to danger before you've had time to name it (Goleman, 1995). Cortisol floods the bloodstream, the prefrontal cortex goes offline, and the body prepares for fight, flight, freeze, or fawn (comply). It doesn't matter whether the threat is physical or emotional. The response is survival. And survival doesn't ask questions.

Jack's triggers are as predictable as they are explosive. Being ignored. Being dismissed. Feeling like his voice doesn't matter. When Lena disengages mid-argument, even to calm herself, he doesn't see space, he sees abandonment. And abandonment, to Jack, is not neutral. It's annihilation.

He was sixteen when his father told him it was time to go. Not in rage, at least, not entirely. In Jack's family, sixteen meant you were old enough to make it on your own. It was a rite of passage disguised as a shove. Go ahead. Walk out. You'll figure it out like the rest of us did. So Jack walked. And no one came after him. No one checked to see if he landed. That wound lives in his body still, not because he left, but because leaving meant no one needed him enough to stop him.

So when Lena pulls away, even in self-preservation, something old and deeply wired rises in him. Not panic. Not rage. Something colder. A hollow certainty. She's done with me. I've already been replaced. And in that split second, he can't bear the stillness. So he fills it, with volume, with control, with anything that reminds him he's still visible.

And when Jack can't stop something, he tries to control it. That's the part he doesn't always see.

Lena's triggers, in contrast, are about proximity. Not connection, enforced proximity. When she feels emotionally cornered, questioned, confronted, pursued without room to breathe, her instinct is to push back. To challenge. To defend her space. But when that pressure doesn't break, when it tightens instead, her system recalibrates. Her voice drops. Her body quiets. She stops resisting, not because she agrees, but because resistance has become unsafe.

Her childhood home was structured, but not stable. Obedience was enforced. Resistance was punished. She learned to read tension like weather. The faster she complied, the fewer the consequences. She became fluent in stillness, but never stopped scanning the exits. Even now, if Jack blocks a doorway, physically or emotionally, her chest tightens with the memory of every time she had no way out.

Her fear isn't theatrical. It's learned. Stored. Automatic.

So when Jack raises his voice, steps in, demands an answer, it doesn't matter what his intention is. Her body doesn't hear a man asking a question. It hears a mother who won't let her leave. And it reacts. She runs, not always with her feet, but with her face, her eyes, her silence. She disappears while standing in the same room.

This is the cruel brilliance of the trauma loop: Jack's fear is that Lena will leave. Lena's fear is that staying will cost her autonomy. And both are trapped in patterns that keep proving the other right.

When Jack escalates, Lena pulls back. When Lena pulls back, Jack escalates.

They aren't reacting to each other. They're reacting to history.

And over time, their roles reversed.

Jack wasn't always the one who avoided hard questions. In the beginning, he asked them. Demanded them. When something felt off, he went after it, intensely, sometimes aggressively. He needed answers, needed closeness, needed to know she wouldn't disappear the way others had. He fought with volume, with urgency, with heat. Because silence, to Jack, meant rejection.

And Lena? She was the one who disappeared.

Not physically, but emotionally. She held her cards close. When things got tense, she shut down. Went quiet. Changed the subject. It wasn't manipulation, it was reflex. In her world, conflict was dangerous, and the safest move was to disengage. So she kept her distance. Measured. Detached. She thought staying calm was staying safe.

But years of volatility flipped their instincts.

Now Lena's the one pushing for truth, clarity, engagement. Because not knowing feels worse than fighting. And Jack? He's the one dodging. The one changing the subject. The one who shuts down or explodes when the questions hit too close. What used to be his pursuit is now her demand. What used to be her silence is now his defense.

That's the adaptation. That's the loop.

They didn't change sides. They changed strategies.

But high-conflict relationships don't stay in one pattern. They adapt.

Years of volatility rewired their survival strategies. Lena, once guarded and withdrawn, now presses in, because being kept in the dark feels more dangerous than confrontation. Jack, once emotionally insistent, now dodges, because being questioned feels like being stripped of control. He avoids the very transparency he used to crave. She chases the very answers she used to fear.

Fearful-avoidants don't just toggle between connection and withdrawal. They flip.

And what once looked like a perfect mismatch, one pushing, one pulling, has become a standoff. A reversal. A reshuffling of armor. Jack uses silence to shield his shame. Lena uses pursuit to avoid emotional erasure. And both believe the other is doing the damage.

What they're caught in isn't just a pattern. It's a conflict echo chamber, a relational loop where each partner's trauma response amplifies the other's. One pushes because they feel ignored. The other retreats because they feel cornered. The more one demands, the more the other withdraws. And the more one withdraws, the more the other presses. It doesn't always matter who starts it, only that the pattern repeats. Not because they're cruel. Not because they don't care. But because each is trying to survive something that no longer exists, except in their bodies, where the past still lives like it just happened.

Their fights don't escalate faster now because the issues are bigger. They escalate faster because both of them are worn thin. The margin is gone. The warning signs are old news. The fuse is shorter than it used to be, and neither of them trusts the other to diffuse it before it burns through.

They don't need new communication tools. They need new nervous systems. And until those change, or until someone chooses to step off the loop, they'll keep replaying the same pain with new dialogue.

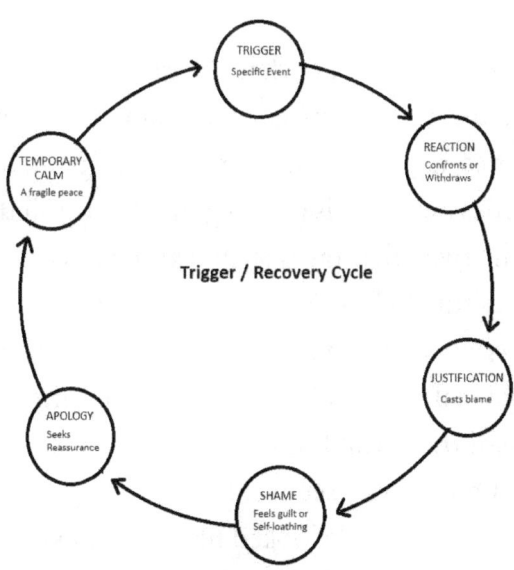

When Shame Becomes Self-Pity — The Subtle Sabotage of Accountability

Jack doesn't know when his shame started speaking louder than Lena's pain. It wasn't a choice. It didn't feel like a shift. It felt like a collapse, of pride, of certainty, of any sense that he was still the man he wanted to be.

He hates what he does when they fight. That much is true. The escalation, the volume, the way he grabs at the emotional wheel as if sheer force will stop her from pulling away. And when it's over, when the silence settles and he's left staring at what's broken, he turns on himself with the same intensity he just aimed at her. I'm awful. I wreck everything. I can't keep doing this.

He doesn't think about what she felt. Not yet. His mind goes to the mess, the damage, the shame, and how to pull himself out of it. And somewhere in that spiral, her side of the story fades because his own regret takes up all the space.

This is the twist that takes shame and bends it into something less useful. Jack isn't using his remorse to understand Lena's experience. He's using it to beat himself up. And in doing so, he makes himself the center of the aftermath. Not the fight. Not the harm. Him.

At first, Lena didn't see it. She mistook Jack's self-condemnation for insight. It looked like depth, like growth. He seemed wrecked by what he'd done, and in her mind, that meant he saw it. That he was closer to changing. So she stayed.

She didn't hold him. Didn't reassure. Just watched, guarded, waiting to see if regret would turn into anything real.

She thought staying might help him see. That if she didn't run, maybe he'd sit with what just happened. But what she didn't realize was that even her silence could be mistaken for mercy.

Because when shame is met with no consequence, it becomes a shortcut. Jack didn't mean to use her that way, but he did. He started to rely on the moment after the storm, when she didn't leave, didn't speak, didn't resist. To him, that meant they were okay. Still bonded. Still salvageable.

But over time, Lena began to feel it, that subtle shift where his remorse wasn't about the damage done, but the redemption he needed. The deeper he fell into guilt, the more he waited for her to pull him out. And when she didn't? That guilt hardened into blame.

You know I hate this.

I'm not a monster.

Why do you always assume the worst of me?

At some point, those phrases stopped sounding like regret and started sounding like a defense. Lena couldn't name it right away. But she felt it, the way his pain filled the room, leaving no space for hers. The way he watched her, not to see what she needed, but to see if he was still worthy in her eyes.

It's a subtle thing, the line between staying present and being used as proof that everything's fine. Lena didn't comfort men through their shame. That was never her instinct. But she'd lingered before, stayed quiet, stayed close, and watched her silence get reinterpreted as forgiveness.

So she stopped staying close at all.

Not out of cruelty. Out of clarity.

She needed to see if Jack's remorse could hold its own. If it meant anything without an audience. Without proximity. Without her presence doing the emotional heavy lifting. Because even just being there, if she wasn't careful, became part of the script he used to avoid changing.

Jack didn't take it well.

He didn't yell. He didn't beg. But something shifted the moment she didn't reach for him. No comfort. No soft landing. Just distance. And in that space, his shame hardened into something else. Not *I hurt her*, but *Why is she still angry? Why won't she let it go?*

Because for Jack, his identity as a "good man" isn't up for debate. He can live with being volatile, even reckless. But not bad. Not unforgivable. So when Lena pulls back instead of leaning in, he doesn't just feel guilt. He feels exposed. Unanchored. Like the script broke halfway through and now there's no clean exit.

It's hard to sit in that space and not flinch. So he flinches. He pushes back.

You know I'm trying. You know I hate this. You know I'm not like that.

And in doing so, he shifts the ground beneath them. Lena, who began as the harmed party, is now being drawn into defending his character. She's not going for it. She's not softening. She's not stepping in to reassure him that he's still a good man. Lena can hold space for remorse, real remorse, the kind that pushes a person toward change. But self-pity? That's where she draws the line. The moment Jack starts spiraling into *I'm the worst, I ruin everything*, she checks out. She's done pushing her own pain aside to make room for his. If he wants comfort, he can earn it with change. Otherwise, he can sit with what he's created, alone.

It's not always intentional. But it works.

That's the trap of self-pity, it wears the face of remorse but reroutes the emotional labor. It shifts the weight. Turns the one who was hurt into the one who's supposed to help. It reframes comfort as obligation.

Lena has started to feel that shift press against her choices. She doesn't want to hurt Jack. She doesn't enjoy watching him spiral. But she refuses to become the answer to pain she didn't cause. Every time she softens without seeing change, something in her stiffens afterward. She goes quieter. Less trusting. Less inclined to reach out. She won't sacrifice her self-respect at the alter of whatever this is.

Because Jack's pain is real.

But so is hers. And only one of them seems to notice when hers gets erased.

And when only one of them gets to feel it, the relationship becomes lopsided. Heavy on one side. Fragile on the other.

Jack doesn't mean to center himself. But his shame is loud. And Lena has learned that her silence will always yield more room. She has spent enough time inside his remorse to know what it needs. What it fears. What it demands.

But she's done carrying it for him.

She still loves him. Still sees the good man beneath the volatility. But she also knows that self-loathing is no substitute for self-control. And until Jack learns to sit in his shame without needing her to clean it up, she will not mistake collapse for growth.

Not again.

Shame isn't the enemy, it's a necessary step toward change. But when it's used to elicit comfort instead of accountability, it stops being vulnerable and starts being strategic. In Jack's case, remorse becomes a detour, not a destination, redirecting the spotlight away from Lena's pain and back onto his need for redemption. And that shift, however unintentional, quietly rewrites the story: from what he did to how bad he feels about it.

Lena's Emotional Withdrawal – A Survival Response, Not a Punishment

Lena never meant for her silence to feel like rejection. In the beginning, she talked. Explained. Debriefed. Tried to walk Jack through her inner world so he could see where he'd crossed the line and why it mattered. She believed, back then, that understanding would change him. That if she could just say it right, calmly enough, clearly enough, he'd stop mistaking her boundaries for threats.

But it didn't work that way.

The more she explained, the more he demanded explanations. The more she offered clarity, the more he mistook it for compliance. Her voice became a tool he relied on, not to understand her, but to stabilize himself. And eventually, Lena realized she wasn't having conversations. She was managing crises. She was narrating her survival.

So now, she doesn't say much after the storm. She walks away. Leaves the room. Turns inward. She's not punishing Jack, but protecting herself from a loop she no longer believes in.

Because she knows the pattern by heart: apology → comfort → hope → escalation.

It always starts with softness. Jack's apology is quiet, sometimes tearful. He reaches for her, not aggressively, but with reverence, like she's something he's scared to lose. He says all the right things, and for a moment, she wants to believe them. She wants to believe that this time, the hurt meant something.

But it's not long before the next trigger arrives. And with it, the return of the storm.

So Lena has stopped following the arc of hope. She is choosing interruption over restoration. She hasn't given up on Jack, but she refuses to be lulled by the illusion of safety that always follows volatility.

Her body doesn't trust peace when it comes too soon. When Jack moves from collapse to comfort-seeking without first sitting in the wreckage, something inside her locks down. Her nervous system recognizes the rhythm. She's been here before, offered forgiveness too soon, leaned in too fast, only to be blindsided when the cycle reset itself with even more velocity.

When Jack apologizes, Lena doesn't automatically reach back. She doesn't soften, doesn't fold. Her survival system no longer links closeness with safety. In fact, it often treats closeness after escalation as a threat. A trap. A lure into the same vulnerability that's been weaponized against her too many times.

She's not cold. She's not cruel. She's just tired.

Tired of being the one who smooths the edges. Tired of cushioning Jack's fall with her presence. Tired of offering comfort as a down payment on future peace that never arrives. What he sees as distance, she experiences as self-preservation. Because emotional closeness isn't neutral anymore, it carries a cost.

And she's decided to stop paying it.

Jack doesn't understand this. Not fully. Her silence unnerves him. He reads it as a message, a tactic, a quiet punishment. He doesn't realize she's not doing anything to him. She's refusing to do what she always did. That's different. That's not cruelty, it's absence.

But absence speaks volumes.

In the quiet that follows a fight, Jack used to reach for her and find her there, wary, yes, but present. Now, she's just… not. Maybe she's in the next room. Maybe she's physically close but emotionally sealed off. Either way, she's no longer his reassurance. No longer the mirror that reflects his regret back as proof of redemption.

She's reclaimed that mirror. Turned it inward.

And Jack, left alone with himself, feels the vacuum.

What he hears in that vacuum is judgment. But that's not what it is. Lena's silence isn't a verdict. It's a boundary. It's the decision not to keep giving beyond her limit. She doesn't owe him emotional regulation while he's learning to manage his own. She doesn't owe him immediate forgiveness just because he hates what he did. And she definitely doesn't owe him the comfort of proximity when proximity feels like exposure.

This is a new edge for her. One that wavers, but holds.

Because withdrawal isn't the same as detachment. Lena still cares. Still loves. Still hopes, on some buried level, that Jack will find his way out of the spiral. But she's stopped sacrificing herself on the altar of that hope. She knows what it costs. And she knows that every time she rushes back in too quickly, she teaches him that collapse is enough. That recovery is a given. That pain is a reset button, not a line that must not be crossed again.

So she doesn't rush anymore.

She lets the silence stretch. Lets the discomfort linger. Opens the door for him to sit with the echo of what happened, not just how it made him feel, but what it did to her. The trust it shook. The space it stole. The part of her that now guards itself even in his gentlest moments.

Because once your body stops feeling safe in someone's presence, it doesn't care how sorry they are.

It cares what they do next.

And until Jack does something different, consistently, repeatedly, Lena will keep choosing space. Not as punishment. As proof that she still belongs to herself.

Lena lay beside him, her back to his chest, eyes wide open in the dark. She could feel the warmth of his body behind her, steady and familiar. Too familiar. He hadn't said anything since the apology, just curled into silence like it was a place he could hide.

She counted his breaths.

Inhale. Exhale. Inhale. Exhale.

She used to wait for his voice in these moments. Wanted to believe that if he reached for her, if he said the right thing, they could rewind the damage, just enough to feel close again. But tonight, she wasn't hoping. She was measuring. Not the time. Not his words.

Her own distance.

Each quiet minute was a marker of clarity. She wasn't waiting for the right words.

She was listening for the moment she no longer needed them.

Breaking the Reflex

This is where the real work begins, not in changing how Jack and Lena fight, but why. Not the surface-level arguments, but the deeper fears driving them: Jack's dread of losing control, Lena's dread of losing herself.

Jack is beginning to understand that remorse isn't the finish line, it's the starting point. Feeling bad isn't enough. He must learn to stay present without overpowering, to feel shame without asking Lena to carry it for him.

Lena, meanwhile, is facing her own question. She never doubted Jack's love for her, but she questioned whether trust could be rebuilt after being shattered again and again. Whether hope is still wise, or just costly.

They both now see that emotional triggers explain harm, but don't excuse it. What trauma uncovers must still be repaired. And what's broken in fear must be healed by deliberate choice.

One night, not long after the last rupture, Jack started to snap again. Voice rising, body tense, words on the edge.

And then, they didn't come.

Just one breath. His jaw tightened. His hands opened. He stayed still.

Lena didn't move either.

It wasn't a breakthrough. But it wasn't another collapse.

It was a pause.

And for them, that pause might be the bravest thing yet.

Chapter Eight

The Recalibration Process – Finding the Right Balance

Progress doesn't arrive with fanfare. It doesn't unfold in bold declarations or sweeping apologies. More often, it slips in quietly, through restraint, through choices made in silence, through the absence of what used to erupt.

Jack didn't decide to change all at once. There was no defining moment, no dramatic vow. Just effort, clumsy, inconsistent, often unnoticed. Sometimes, he catches himself before the escalation. Sometimes, he walks away to avoid losing control. It's not mastery. But it's movement.

Lena sees the difference. She sees the pauses where fire used to live. But she doesn't rush in with softness. She doesn't mistake restraint for reliability. Instead, she waits. Not coldly, but carefully. Because she's learned that one good moment doesn't promise the next.

This chapter is about that in-between space, the fragile territory between old patterns and something not yet proven. Jack is learning to sit in discomfort without using power to soothe it. Lena is learning to sit in silence without stepping in to manage his pain. And in this unspoken shift, something new begins.

Not peace. Not resolution.

Just a recalibration, tentative, uneven, and real.

False Starts and Fragile Progress

Jack didn't slam the door this time.

He could have. The moment practically begged for it. Lena had just said something about his brother, a topic he considered sacred territory, and the air between them had shifted like the pressure drop before a storm. His face had already changed, she could tell. The flare in his eyes, the subtle roll of his shoulders like he was resetting for battle. Every cue told her to brace for impact.

But he didn't lash out. He didn't even raise his voice. He just turned, walked out of the room, and left the door open behind him.

It wasn't a performance. It wasn't a strategic withdrawal meant to punish her with silence. He was regulating, trying, at least. Outside, she heard the wooden creak of the porch steps as he paced back and forth, shoes scuffing with a kind of desperate rhythm. A loop. Tight. Repetitive. Like his thoughts.

Inside, she stood still. Waiting, not fearfully, but carefully. Alert in the way someone becomes when they're watching an animal that could be either wounded or dangerous. She hadn't expected a blow. Jack hadn't hurt her in that way since the night everything almost ended. But still. Old patterns have long shadows. She didn't move toward the door. She didn't go check on him. She didn't fill the silence with soft edges or reach for closeness.

Instead, she waited. Like a scientist.

She observed.

Jack was changing, yes, but change wasn't the same as stability. It wasn't the same as safety. It was effort. It was mess. It was the difference between a man holding himself back and a man who no longer needed to.

When he came back in, his voice was even. Still tight, but measured. He said, "I'm not going to talk about him right now," and nothing more. No demand, no accusation. He sat down at the far edge of the couch like he was giving her space, or maybe taking it for himself.

She gave a small nod and returned to her book, eyes scanning lines she wasn't reading.

The moment passed. Nobody won. Nobody lost. And for the first time in a long time, that felt like progress.

But not the kind of progress Lena could trust.

Because when a man like Jack holds back, you feel the tension in the space he leaves behind. You feel the words he doesn't say. You feel the doorframe that didn't rattle, the volume that didn't rise. And you can't help but wonder: Was it because he's learning... or because he's afraid of what he might do?

Jack's effort was real. She knew that. He wasn't coasting or faking it. He had started to name his triggers, the particular cocktail of pressure, helplessness, and exposure that set him off like a match to dry pine. He knew the signs. He could sometimes catch them. But not always. And even when he did, the aftermath was like watching a man bite down on his own instincts without knowing if the teeth would hold.

He told her once, in one of those rare, honest moments, "I don't know how to walk away without feeling like I lost." He hadn't said it proudly. It was a confession. A problem he didn't yet know how to solve.

It made sense. Jack's history had taught him that control was protection, that power meant safety. Letting someone else dictate the terms of a conversation, especially one that touched his shame, wasn't just uncomfortable. It was existentially threatening. When he backed down, he didn't just feel embarrassed. He felt erased. Forgotten. Like every word he didn't say would vanish into Lena's memory of him as weak, unworthy, irrelevant.

And relevance, for Jack, was everything.

Lena saw all of this. She understood it. But understanding didn't make it her responsibility anymore.

That was the difference.

In the early years, when Jack's volatility would rise like a summer storm, fast, hot, and violent, Lena had made it her job to soothe him. She feared that if she didn't say the right thing, or stay calm enough, he'd spin into something even more dangerous. She'd learned to moderate the climate. To keep things cool enough to survive.

But now? Now she didn't rush to fix the weather. She didn't offer comforting words just because he'd managed not to explode. She didn't reach for his hand to reward him for basic restraint. That wasn't cynicism. It was caution. She needed to know that Jack could make a better choice without being rescued by her softness.

Because if she stepped in every time he almost unraveled, then the change wouldn't belong to him, it would belong to her.

So she stayed still. Neutral. Kind, but not encouraging. Present, but not emotionally available in the way she used to be.

Jack noticed. Of course he did. He didn't say anything directly, but his silences grew heavier. He'd pace more. Mutter things under his breath. Try to bait her with low-level provocations, subtle enough to pass as offhanded but weighted with intention. She knew that game. Push her just enough to get her to reengage, to say something, to feel something. To pull him back into the intimacy of conflict.

But she wouldn't play.

Not because she didn't care, but because she did.

This was the cost of real change. It was a price they both had to pay.

Letting go of the dynamic they both knew so well meant stepping into a space where neither of them had scripts. No rhythm. No predictable resolution. Just silence and tension and the slow, frustrating process of becoming different people in the same room.

And it was hard.

Sometimes Lena questioned her own motives. Was she withholding? Being cold? Using emotional distance to punish him for the past? But when she really sat with it, she knew the truth: she wasn't punishing. She was protecting. Not from Jack, exactly, but from the inertia of slipping back into the person she used to be around him.

Because the woman who calmed Jack's storms was brave, yes, but also exhausted. She gave too much. She absorbed too much. And every time she managed his volatility, she lost a little more of her own center.

So now she held the line. Let him feel the weight of his restraint. Let him sit in the silence he used to fill with shouting.

And Jack?

He sat there too.

Not always well. Not always gracefully. But he stayed. He endured his own unease, even when it clawed at his insides. Even when his pride screamed at him to do something, say something, win something.

He stayed.

It wasn't triumph. It wasn't healing. But it was something. And that something mattered more than any apology he could offer.

Because restraint isn't just an act, it's a recalibration of the entire nervous system. Especially for someone like Jack, whose body had long equated intensity with survival.

And Lena, watching, waiting, wary, understood the difference.

He hadn't exploded. He hadn't walked out to punish. He hadn't turned her fear into fuel for his rage.

And she hadn't stepped in to save him.

Not this time.

Not anymore.

What Jack Believes About Power

Jack didn't know how to stop without disappearing.

That was the thing about power, he didn't just crave it. He didn't even want it, not in the traditional sense. It was more primitive than that. He needed it, the way a drowning man needs the surface. It wasn't about control so much as visibility. Presence. Proof that he mattered.

In his world, presence had always been earned through pressure. You made yourself loud enough, firm enough, relentless enough to be taken seriously. Fear was a kind of currency. And Jack had learned early that you either held it or paid it.

The first time he understood what that meant, he was seven. His brother, eight years older, had just come back from a fight behind the high school gym. Jack remembered the blood still wet on his brother's shirt, a gash above his eye that looked like it belonged in a movie. His father didn't yell. Didn't scold. Just nodded once and muttered, "Good. If they fear you, they'll never forget you."

That line stuck.

Jack repeated it to himself years later when his voice first cracked with rage in front of a girlfriend who threatened to leave. He didn't hit her. Didn't even touch her. But he'd roared, loud and guttural, and watched her flinch so hard she nearly dropped her keys. Afterward, he apologized, of course. Promised it wouldn't happen again. But some quiet part of him noted that she stayed.

She'd seen what he was capable of. And she'd stayed.

It worked.

Or at least, it felt like it did.

Now, years later, Lena wasn't playing by those rules. She didn't stay because he was loud. She didn't back down when he puffed up. In fact, the more he tried to dominate the conversation, the more detached she became. It wasn't passive resistance. It was refusal. Not a fight. Not a surrender. Just a slow, deliberate exit from the game entirely.

It unmoored him.

Because if conflict was no longer a doorway back into closeness, what was it?

If raising his voice didn't get her to re-engage, didn't remind her how important he was, then what purpose did it serve?

Worse, who was he without it?

Jack didn't fear being wrong. He feared being irrelevant. And when Lena disengaged mid-conflict, when she folded her arms and let him spiral without chasing or collapsing, it felt like erasure. She was deliberately refusing to prove she cared by matching his fire.

And that, more than anything, scared him.

So now, when he tried to do it right, when he caught himself before the explosion, the silence that followed felt unbearable. Not because it was hostile. Lena wasn't cold. She wasn't punishing. But she was distant. Watchful. No longer drawn into the emotional orbit of his spirals. She let him choose something different. And she let him sit with it.

He sat with it like a man sitting in a room after a bomb has been defused. Nothing detonated. Nothing destroyed. But the tension still buzzed in the walls, waiting.

He was supposed to be proud of himself. And on some level, he was. But pride didn't taste the way he thought it would. It tasted like defeat. Like surrender. Like standing down when every part of him had been trained to strike.

Because he still believed, at least reflexively, that control was survival.

Jack could say the right things. "I know yelling doesn't help." "I don't want to be that guy." "I'm trying to stay calm." But underneath it, in the marrow of his bones, calm still felt like weakness. Like giving up territory. Like letting someone else define the moment.

The worst part? He couldn't even say it out loud. Not to Lena. Especially not to her.

Because what kind of man admits that losing his temper makes him feel more real?

He didn't want to be that man anymore. He really didn't. But when the heat rose in his chest, when the accusation slipped past her lips, when her tone turned clipped or cold or challenging, his body lit up before his mind could catch it.

It wasn't that he wanted to dominate her. It was that he didn't want to disappear. And somewhere in his past, those two things had been welded together so tightly that pulling them apart now felt like losing pieces of himself.

Cognitive dissonance doesn't always feel like confusion. Sometimes it feels like fire. Jack could know, know, that walking away was the right choice, and still feel like a coward as he did it. He could feel proud and ashamed in the same breath. Because when Lena didn't follow, when she didn't validate his effort, it stirred something deeper. Something older.

The belief that if you're not feared, you're forgotten.

It wasn't rational. It wasn't even conscious most of the time. But it lived in him. In the way his voice would rise half a step before he caught it. In the way his shoulders would tense when she refused to argue. In the flicker of resentment that sparked when she walked away instead of engaging.

She did that now.

Walked away.

Not out of spite. Not because she'd given up. But because she refused to become the audience to a performance she'd seen too many times before.

He watched her go, shoulders straight, spine long, her back to him without hesitation.

And there it was. That familiar wave of threat. Not from her. From the emptiness she left behind.

He flexed his hands, open, closed, open again. His jaw tightened and released. He wanted to call her name, to drag the moment back into something familiar. To do something. Win something.

But he didn't.

He stood in the kitchen, surrounded by the echo of a silence he didn't know how to live in. Not yet.

Because silence had always meant exile in his world. Distance meant danger. If someone wasn't yelling, they were disappearing. If someone wasn't in the fight, they'd already left.

And yet, Lena hadn't left. She was still here. Just not playing the game.

That's what terrified him most.

She was calling his bluff, not to hurt him, but to free herself. And maybe, if he could survive the discomfort, to free him too.

But freedom requires surrender. And Jack had only ever known how to take.

So he stayed where he was. Jaw tight. Hands twitching. Still.

And for once, he let the moment pass because he knew that if he didn't, the man he was trying to become would vanish beneath the man he'd always been.

The Moment of Truth – A Historical Escalation Replayed

It started with a question, too direct, too loaded, the kind that always made Jack feel cornered.

They'd just finished dinner. No tension in the air yet. Lena had been quiet most of the evening, thoughtful in that way that made Jack's stomach knot even before she spoke. She waited until the plates were rinsed and stacked. No audience. No distractions.

Then: "Why didn't you tell me what your mom said that night?"

She didn't raise her voice. Didn't accuse. Just asked.

But Jack's breath caught anyway.

Not because of the question itself, he'd been asked harder things by people who mattered less, but because of what it threatened to open. That night. His silence. The memory of sitting frozen, staring out the window as the sky went dark, listening to his mother spit venom about the woman he loved. Words he could never unsay, even if Lena never heard them. He thought he was protecting her. Maybe he still believed that.

So he defaulted.

"I told you. She was having one of her episodes."

A deflection. Clean. Easy. Enough to move on.

But Lena didn't move.

She tilted her head slightly, brows drawn, not angry, but anchored. "Your sister said the ambulance came. That you wouldn't ride with her. That it was about...me."

Jack stiffened. His fingers twitched at his sides.

"She wasn't trying to stir anything up," Lena added quietly. "It just came out when we were talking about family stuff."

Still, the damage was done.

"Don't bring her into this," Jack said flatly.

Lena didn't flinch. "I'm not. I'm asking you."

Her voice was steady. Tired, but steady.

"I already know how she feels about me," she said. "You weren't shielding me from the truth. You were trying to keep me from hearing it *from you.*"

And there it was. The match to the kindling.

His vision narrowed. His heartbeat thickened in his throat. This was the place where he used to explode, where the words would fly, the volume would rise, the room would shrink to the size of his fury. He could already feel the heat in his chest, the squeeze behind his eyes. All the old signals were firing. Same spark. Same fuel.

But then something shifted.

It wasn't clarity. It wasn't calm. It was recognition. Jack saw it happening, saw himself happening, and for the first time, he didn't follow the script.

He walked outside.

Not to slam the door. Not to make her chase him. But because he knew what came next, and he didn't want to live through it again.

The air outside was sharp. Not cold, but biting enough to pull his attention away from the chaos in his head. He paced. Five steps one way, five back. The gravel underfoot crunched with every turn. His hands opened and closed at his sides, palms flexing like he could squeeze the heat out of them.

His chest tightened. He wanted to scream. To punch something. To demand that she take it back, that she admit she was wrong for confronting him like that, that she see how hard he was trying and stop pushing. He wanted to make her feel what he felt. Just for a second.

But he didn't.

Instead, he breathed. Shallow at first, then deeper. He watched the pattern of his own pacing. Tried to feel the edges of his body instead of the fire inside it. His jaw ached from clenching, but he didn't open his mouth.

He stayed out there until the wave crested. Until the thrum in his chest started to dull. Until he could hear more than the scream inside his own skull.

Inside the house, Lena didn't move.

She didn't follow. Didn't text. Didn't wait by the door.

She sat on the edge of the couch, legs crossed, hands tucked into her lap. Alert, but still. Holding her own center the way she used to hold his.

She didn't feel relief, not yet. Relief would be premature. He hadn't earned it. Not fully. But she noticed what hadn't happened. Noticed the door that didn't slam. The scream that didn't come. The weight of his presence moving away instead of bearing down on her.

And that meant something. Not everything. But something.

When Jack came back inside, his face was pale, jaw still tight. But his eyes were clear. Focused. Not soft, but not wild, either.

He stood by the entryway, fingers twitching slightly at his sides.

"I didn't tell you," he said quietly, "because I didn't know how to talk about it. I still don't."

That was it. No apology. No grand explanation. But no attack either.

Lena didn't reach for him. She didn't fill the silence. She just nodded once, a small, deliberate gesture that said I heard you, and returned her gaze to the floor.

The moment passed.

No explosion. No reparation. Just space.

Unfinished. Unresolved. But not undone.

And that was the miracle.

Because the old Jack wouldn't have walked away. The old Jack would've doubled down, demanded submission, turned his shame into fire and set the whole room ablaze.

But this time, he didn't.

This time, the fire stayed inside.

And for Jack, that restraint didn't feel like growth. It felt like collapse. Like standing on legs that hadn't yet learned how to bear the weight of a new identity. Like waiting for Lena to come to him, and feeling the ache of her stillness like a wound.

But she didn't come. She didn't rescue him. She didn't reward the moment.

And maybe that was the most loving thing she could've done.

Because real progress doesn't come with applause. It doesn't feel triumphant. It feels anticlimactic. Empty. Quiet.

It feels like surviving the thing you thought would destroy you, and then sitting in the silence afterward, wondering if it was enough.

Testing vs. Trusting – Lena's New Role

Lena used to meet fire with fire.

Not always. Not proudly. But in those early years, when Jack's rage came fast and hot, she discovered that flinching made things worse. Softness, too. If she tried to stay calm, he took it as resistance. If she folded, he saw weakness. But if she pushed back, loudly, sharply, with the same teeth he bared, he paused. Not because she'd hurt him, but because he recognized the energy. It was survival language. Primitive, ugly, familiar.

So she learned to hold her ground by striking first. Matching tone for tone. Throwing words like darts just to keep from feeling cornered. It wasn't about dominance, it was about not drowning in someone else's storm.

And it worked, until it didn't.

Until she realized that winning the argument only meant they'd both lost something else.

Now, everything was different. Or trying to be. Jack was trying. He really was. The explosions were fewer. Shorter. Less venomous. Sometimes they didn't happen at all.

But that didn't mean Lena felt safe.

Because safety, for her, had never come from silence. It had come from control. From reading the emotional climate before it broke. From managing Jack's volatility like a full-time job. The danger wasn't just in his anger, it was in the unpredictability of it. If she could predict it, she could survive it. And if she could control it, she could almost pretend it wasn't happening.

Now, she wasn't doing that anymore.

She wasn't smoothing things over. Wasn't diffusing tension with warmth or humor or calculated calm. She wasn't performing emotional CPR after every near-escalation.

Instead, she was doing something harder.

She was waiting.

Letting Jack regulate himself. Letting him decide what kind of man he wanted to be, not through pressure or persuasion, but through silence. Through observation.

And it cost her more than she let on.

Not because stillness was unfamiliar. Lena knew how to go quiet. She'd survived most of her life by withdrawing just far enough to stay untouched. But not managing Jack, that was different. That was new.

She wasn't used to seeing someone she loved spiral and doing nothing to stop it. Not used to letting silence speak when she had the words that might soften the edge. She knew how to step in. How to read his temperature, adjust hers, steer them both back to stable ground.

But now she was choosing not to.

Letting him flail. Letting him figure it out. Watching him ache without offering comfort, because she needed the next move to be his.

That kind of holding back doesn't feel like empowerment. It feels like betrayal. Like failing someone you love on purpose. Like walking a tightrope between cruelty and self-preservation. Sometimes she asked herself if she was being cruel. If her silence was punishment dressed up as self-protection. If she was withholding love in a moment when Jack needed it most.

But deep down, she knew that wasn't it.

She wasn't cold. She was cautious.

Because she'd seen this pattern before, he explodes, she reacts, he apologizes, she forgives. The cycle spins, the roles stay the same, and nothing really changes.

This time, she needed to know if the silence would hold.

One night, not long after the conversation about Jack's mother, he came to her softly. No preamble. No defensiveness.

He sat beside her on the couch, a good three feet of space between them, and said, "I didn't handle that well. I'm not proud of how I shut down. But I didn't want to hurt you."

His voice was level. Not rehearsed. Not manipulative. He wasn't fishing for comfort. He was offering a repair.

And Lena wanted to meet him there. She wanted to lean in, to bridge the gap, to tell him she saw his effort and appreciated it.

But she didn't.

Not yet.

She nodded, eyes on the floor, and said, "Okay."

Not dismissive. Not hostile. Just... careful.

Because she'd learned that moments like this don't mean the cycle is broken. They mean it's paused. Interrupted. And interruptions only matter if they're repeated. If they become pattern. If they hold under pressure.

So she waited.

Not to test him, but to protect herself.

She'd believed him before. Believed that things were changing, that the worst was behind them. But belief, she'd learned, was a kind of currency she couldn't afford to spend too quickly.

Jack noticed the distance. She could feel it in the way he shifted beside her, the brief twitch in his fingers like he wanted to reach out but wasn't sure if he was allowed to. She didn't stop him. But she didn't move closer, either.

This was the new equation: Jack reached, and Lena held.

The role reversal was clear now. Jack was no longer the one demanding distance; he was the one asking for connection. And Lena, the pursuer, the empath, the fixer, was holding the boundary.

Not forever. Not rigidly. But firmly enough to know that if this change was real, it would show itself again. Without coaxing. Without her stepping in to make it easier.

Because love isn't just about reunion after rupture. It's about how many ruptures you're willing to endure before you stop trusting the repair.

She wanted a partner who could hold his own emotional temperature. Who didn't need her to regulate the climate every time things got heated. Who didn't melt down the moment she asked a question that scraped too close to the bone.

She didn't want to be Jack's mirror anymore.

Didn't want to be the soft edge that kept him from seeing himself clearly. If he was growing, if he was learning to de-escalate, to take responsibility, to sit with his own shame instead of turning it into rage, then he needed to do it without her applause.

Trust isn't born from a single moment of restraint. It's born from repetition. Consistency. The kind of slow, deliberate rebuilding that doesn't announce itself.

And Jack's gesture, sincere though it was, didn't prove anything yet.

It was a beginning. Nothing more.

Lena wanted to believe. But belief had to be earned. Not by grand gestures, but by quiet, ordinary choices made over and over again.

So she waited. Again.

She cared differently now. Care used to look like managing him. Now, it looked like holding him accountable.

That shift cost her more than she let on. There were nights she lay awake, wondering if she was being too hard. If she was pushing him away just when he was trying to come closer. If the part of her that had always needed to be in control was winning over the part that longed to trust again.

But then she'd remember the years of chaos. The nights she curled inward while he paced outside, the fights that ended with apologies and empty promises. The way hope had worn her down into something brittle and tired.

And she'd remember that this version of her, the one who stayed still, who didn't chase, who let silence speak, wasn't heartless.

She was healing.

The Pattern Breaks, but the Pattern Watches

The next conflict came before either of them was ready.

It was nothing, really. One of those ordinary moments that turns into something else, not because of what was said, but because of what it stirred.

Lena had asked if Jack was still planning to call his sister about the paperwork. Calm, offhanded, no edge in her voice.

Jack tensed before she even finished the sentence.

He hadn't called. He didn't want to talk about it. And he didn't want to explain why, especially not after the week they'd just had. The near-miss. The self-restraint. The quiet standoff on the couch that somehow counted as a win.

And now she was bringing it up again.

"I'll get to it," he said.

"You said that two days ago."

His chest tightened. "I said I'll handle it."

There it was. The shift.

His voice wasn't loud. Not yet. But it had grown in size, taken up more space than the words required. His posture changed too: shoulders squared, jaw locked, eyes fixed just a little too hard.

Lena froze.

Not visibly. Not dramatically. Just enough to signal that old fear of what this might become.

Jack saw it. The subtle draw back of her body. The way her arms folded in, almost like a shield. It hit him harder than the words had.

She was afraid of the pattern, not the moment.

And that, somehow, felt worse.

He took a breath, sharp and audible. His body still buzzing with the remnants of adrenaline. His throat tight with everything he didn't want to say.

Then, quietly, "I'm sorry."

Not the kind that erases things. Just the kind that means I saw it too.

"I got loud. I know."

Lena nodded once. Said nothing.

And that silence, that lack of reaction, told him more than any argument would have.

Because she was watching now. Not judging, not punishing. But watching. Waiting to see if this moment would become another crack in the foundation, or if it would settle without damage.

It was hard to say.

The volume hadn't exploded. The fight hadn't escalated. He hadn't crossed any lines. But he'd brushed against them, and for someone like Jack, that brush was enough to raise the question again: Is this who I still am?

He backed off. Literally. Took a step toward the door, then changed his mind. He didn't want to run from the discomfort. But he also didn't want to sit in it with her gaze on him.

So he left the room, not with the weight of shame, but with the weight of consequence.

Later that night, he sat alone in the back room, the one with the low light and the chair that creaked if you leaned the wrong way. No music. No TV. Just the soft hum of the air system and the echo of his own voice playing the scene back again and again.

He hadn't exploded. But he'd almost done it.

He hadn't said anything cruel. But he'd scared her anyway.

And that, somehow, was the part that broke him open.

Because Jack had always measured progress by what he didn't do. Didn't scream. Didn't grab. Didn't smother. But tonight reminded him that not doing damage isn't the same as doing good. That fear can live in the space between words, in a tone, in a posture, in the heat of a glance.

And Lena, who had been learning to trust the new version of him, had just been reminded that he was still building it.

He rubbed his palms together, then rested them flat against his knees. The motion was grounding, but not comforting. His muscles ached from holding tension that had nowhere to go.

He didn't spiral. Didn't collapse into guilt or defensiveness. But he didn't feel proud, either.

He felt... tired.

Not the kind of tired that sleep fixes. The kind that comes from wrestling something ancient. Something embedded in your nervous system, in your reflexes, in the language your body speaks before your mind catches up.

This was the fight.

Not the one between him and Lena, but the one inside himself. Between instinct and intention. Between the man who had survived by getting big, and the one trying to survive by staying still.

It wasn't a clean win. It wasn't a loss, either.

It was a reminder.

That progress isn't measured in apologies, or even in restraint. It's measured in what happens next. In the choice to return to that same emotional edge, again and again, and step back every time, not once, not twice, but until the edge dulls. Until the body learns a new language. Until the silence after tension doesn't feel like failure, but like peace.

Jack knew now: this wasn't about changing once.

It was about changing under pressure. Repeatedly. Quietly. Without applause.

Until the new choice becomes instinct.

And the old one finally loses its grip.

Holding the Space: What Real Change Feels Like

Real change doesn't always look like growth. Sometimes it looks like stillness, like biting your tongue when every part of you wants to shout. Like walking away without slamming the door. Like sitting with the person you love, saying nothing at all, because neither of you trusts the words just yet.

That's the quiet truth about recalibration: it doesn't feel heroic. It feels awkward, anticlimactic, and sometimes even lonely. The drama is gone, but so is the false intimacy that came with the explosion and repair cycle. What's left is unfamiliar territory, uncharted and unnerving.

If you're in the thick of it, trying to change or walk alongside someone who is, ask yourself: What does real change look like in my life or relationship? Does it feel like progress, or does it feel like waiting? Does it bring peace, or just a different kind of tension?

Try this:

Journal Prompt: Think of a moment where you chose differently. What came before it? What stopped you from slipping into the old pattern? What happened afterward?

Was there relief? Was there silence? Did anyone notice?

Or did it pass like most real victories do, quietly, without ceremony?

There's a moment, late one evening, where Jack and Lena end up on opposite ends of the couch. No fight. No tension in the air. Just the long residue of a hard day. Jack doesn't reach for her. Lena doesn't pull away. They sit in that small, unremarkable space between distance and closeness, where nothing is demanded and nothing is promised.

Outside, the wind taps at the windows. The room is dim except for the kitchen light, left on by accident or habit.

Neither of them speaks.

But neither of them moves.

And in that stillness, there is no war. No repair. No fear.

Just two people learning, slowly, to stay.

Chapter Nine

Can You Change a Partner Who Thrives on Resistance?

Jack hasn't lost control in months.

There are no new holes in the drywall. No doors slammed so hard the hinges cry out. No moments where Lena's body floods with adrenaline before her mind catches up. On paper, this is the kind of progress most people would celebrate. But for Lena, the quiet brings its own kind of unease.

Because control, as it turns out, can wear many faces. Jack doesn't shout anymore, but sometimes he vanishes inside himself, walls up with measured silence that feels no less punishing. He still needs to win, to preserve a sense of dominance over the moment. He's just found subtler ways to do it. And Lena, who used to mark safety by the absence of chaos, is learning that stillness isn't always peace. Sometimes, it's just pressure with the volume turned down.

This chapter is about what happens after the worst moments stop. After apologies have been made and behavioral boundaries have held, but the emotional terrain remains shaky. It's about the fragile hope that comes with early change, the kind that demands constant vigilance but offers no guarantees. And it's about Lena's evolution, too, not just waiting to feel safe, but learning to define what safety actually looks like.

Because progress in a high-conflict relationship is never a single turn. It's a series of choices. Most of them small. Most of them quiet. Most of them invisible to anyone not watching closely.

But Lena is watching. And what she sees now is a man who hasn't been violent in a long time, and who may never be again. But she also sees the tremor beneath the surface. The part of him that still bristles at vulnerability. The part that isn't dangerous right now, but could be, if they stop paying attention.

The Invisible Strain of Self-Restraint

Jack doesn't raise his voice anymore. He doesn't punch the wall or slam doors or grip Lena's wrists in a moment of panic disguised as rage. If you were to walk into their house on a tense evening, you might think it was peaceful. There's no shouting. No obvious signs of a fight. The wine glasses are upright. The dog is asleep on the couch.

But Lena watches him from across the room, and she knows better.

There's a particular way he breathes when he's trying not to break, tight inhale, slow exhale, jaw working like it's chewing on a memory. His hands flex rhythmically at his sides. Not fists, not quite. Just tension searching for an outlet. He says he's "managing it." Lena wonders if he even knows what it is.

This is the version of Jack he's proud of. Controlled. Calm. Quiet. And Lena doesn't dismiss the effort. She knows what it costs him not to erupt. What it takes to pull the brake on an impulse that once ran wild. But she also knows what it's like to be on the receiving end of silence that isn't peace. His restraint, impressive as it may be, carries its own gravity, a dense emotional pressure that fills the room without ever making a sound.

To Jack, not exploding is progress. And in many ways, it is. But he clings to that measure as if it's the only one that matters. If he didn't yell, then he's succeeded. If he didn't grab her arm, then he's changed. If he walked away before the worst part happened, then surely he's safe now. Surely, she can see that.

But Lena doesn't feel safe. She feels... suspended. Like the air between them is holding its breath.

She used to fear his outbursts, when his voice would rise and his presence would fill the room like a storm front, demanding her attention, forcing her into emotional compliance. Now, what she fears is the absence. The empty spaces where dialogue used to be. The long pauses where he should ask, Are you okay? but instead says nothing. It's not that he shuts her down, it's that he no longer opens up. He's taken the chaos off the table, but replaced it with something colder, quieter, harder to name.

Emotional withdrawal can look a lot like maturity from the outside. And for someone like Jack, who used to lash out when threatened, stepping back feels like growth. But Lena knows better. She knows that when he disappears emotionally, it's not out of serenity. It's out of self-preservation. He's not choosing calm, he's avoiding vulnerability. He still needs to win, but now he wins by not engaging. He lets silence be the last word.

Sometimes, when Lena brings something up, a concern, a need, a discomfort, Jack just listens, nods once, and says, "Okay." Then nothing. No reaction, no discussion. Not even resistance. And somehow, that feels worse. Because the old Jack, the volatile Jack, would've argued. He would've fought to make his version of events the dominant one. He would've insisted that her interpretation was flawed, that her feelings were exaggerated, that she was just trying to trap him in a blame game.

Now he doesn't even give her that. He gives her distance. Compliance without connection.

And she doesn't know if that's better.

Jack tells himself that silence is safety. That not reacting is proof of evolution. He believes that walking away from a fight is the same as solving it. In his mind, not breaking things means he's healing. But Lena feels the difference. She feels the withholding. The tension under the surface. Like he's holding his breath and waiting for her to finish feeling something inconvenient.

She doesn't want the old Jack back. She's grateful he doesn't lash out anymore. But she's not comforted by this new version, not entirely. Because Jack doesn't just withhold anger now. He withholds himself. And Lena, who has spent a lifetime learning to decipher the language of emotional threat, recognizes the pattern. It's not calm. It's controlled disengagement. The kind that says, I will not hurt you, but I will not meet you either.

She knows what it feels like to be trapped in an argument. Now she's learning what it feels like to be trapped in an absence of one.

Psychologically, what Jack is doing isn't uncommon in trauma-conditioned men trying to change reactive behaviors. According to Ford and Courtois (2014), individuals with complex trauma often attempt to regulate emotional responses by suppressing affect entirely, especially when they associate expression with danger or shame. The problem is, suppression doesn't equal integration. It's a management strategy, not a transformation. And without deeper healing, those suppressed impulses don't vanish, they wait.

Jack doesn't see this yet. He thinks he's fixed it. But Lena knows better than to mistake quiet for peace. She's lived through too many emotional sleights of hand to be fooled now. The danger isn't in what he does. It's in what he refuses to feel.

Sometimes, he sits on the porch after one of their unresolved conversations, staring out at nothing in particular. His body still. His hands quiet. Lena will pass by the window and glance at him, and in that moment, he looks like a man who's won a small war with himself. And maybe he has. But from the other side of the glass, it doesn't look like victory.

It looks like a man who's decided the only way to keep his partner is to disappear piece by piece, until all that remains is the version he thinks she can tolerate.

And Lena, standing just out of view, wonders how long she can live with a man who no longer fights, but no longer shows up either.

Lena's New Question: Is Love Enough?

Lena never wondered if Jack loved her. Of course he did. That was never in question.

The problem was what he did with that love. How easily it tipped into something possessive, controlling, urgent in all the wrong ways. How quickly it became a justification. I love you always came after the damage, like that made it count more.

What kept her up at night weren't questions about his heart. It was what that heart cost her.

She wasn't looking for reassurance. She was looking for consistency. For love that didn't arrive in pieces, apologies on

Tuesday, silence on Wednesday, tenderness on Thursday like it cancelled the rest out.

She could track his patterns by now. The remorse was predictable. So was the effort. But so was the part where it slipped. She didn't need to know if he felt something for her. She needed to know if those feelings would ever stop turning her into collateral damage.

That's what she was watching now, not his words, not his guilt, not his good intentions. His follow-through.

So yes, she believed he loved her.

Now, the question is different. She asks if that love is safe. If it can stand the weight of their history, the strain of their patterns, the silence that's settled in place of the shouting. If it can evolve past survival and into something that doesn't require her to shape herself around his wounds.

Jack has changed. She won't deny that. The rage that used to crash through the walls of their home like a wrecking ball hasn't shown up in months. He listens more. He pulls back when things get heated. And when he's triggered, he disappears into himself instead of into her space. She knows that's effort. She knows it costs him something. But it's what she is doing now that scares her.

Because somewhere along the line, her role quietly shifted. Where she once protected herself by disengaging, letting his fire burn out on its own, now she finds herself managing him again. Watching for signs. Measuring his tone. Adjusting her language mid-sentence. Not to avoid harm, but to preserve the progress. To keep the fragile structure of their peace from collapsing under the weight of old reflexes.

It's subtle, this vigilance. It hides in small moments: the way she hesitates before asking a difficult question, the way she mentally rehearses how to bring up something he might take as criticism. It's the long pause before she challenges him, not because she fears his rage, but because she dreads the shutdown that follows. The quiet withdrawal. The emotional distance she can't quite cross.

She remembers when the roles were reversed. When Jack was the one trying to pull her in, and she was the one who stayed just out of reach. When she would retreat behind a wall of logic or sarcasm, refusing to let him in because closeness felt like a trap. He'd come to her then, desperate to be seen, to be heard, sometimes demanding it with a force she couldn't handle. She resented it, feared it. And yet, it meant he still wanted her presence, even if he didn't know how to ask for it gently.

Now, she's the one who asks. The one who pursues understanding. And he... disappears.

Not in body. Jack is still there, making coffee, folding towels, sitting next to her on the couch. But something in him has gone quiet. Like he's rationing his emotional bandwidth, afraid that if he feels too much, he'll lose control again. She doesn't blame him. But she's starting to wonder: if she's always the one reaching in, and he's always the one holding back, is this still a relationship, or just damage control?

Lena knows what emotional erasure feels like. It was the atmosphere of her childhood, quiet compliance mistaken for peace, feelings dismissed as weakness, boundaries treated like rebellion. She survived by becoming hyperaware. Learning to read a room before she entered it. Learning to bend just enough to keep herself safe without completely disappearing. But it came at a cost. And now, sitting across from Jack at the kitchen table, watching him retreat behind a neutral expression, she feels that cost creeping in again.

She swore she wouldn't lose herself to this dynamic. That she'd stay if it felt like growth, not sacrifice. But growth is messy. It doesn't arrive with trumpets. It looks like Jack not yelling when he wants to. Like Lena biting her tongue when she wants to scream, *Engage with me, damn it!* It looks like two people trying to rebuild something neither of them fully understands.

And maybe that's the problem. Jack sees love as effort. As staying. As not hurting her. And Lena, once comforted by those markers, now sees something more complicated. Because the way he avoids escalation also allows him to avoid intimacy. He doesn't push her anymore, but he doesn't meet her either. He retreats to a kind of emotional arm's length where nothing gets damaged, but nothing gets touched.

Attachment theory speaks to this dynamic. In fearful-avoidant individuals, especially those with trauma histories, there is often a push-pull between the longing for connection and the fear of being consumed or rejected by it (Levine & Heller, 2010). Jack's newfound restraint may serve as a shield against the shame of past failures, but it also becomes a barrier to genuine closeness. And Lena, equally avoidant but conditioned to survive through vigilance, recognizes the trap: she is once again becoming the moderator of his emotional landscape.

That's the question she can't stop circling: If I'm the one keeping the connection alive, is it still mutual?

There's a loneliness in this new silence. Not the explosive kind, the kind that rattles your bones and forces you to flee, but a quieter ache. One that comes from being next to someone who says he's trying but won't let you see the trying. Who says he's present but stays hidden beneath a practiced calm. She misses the fire, not because she wants the pain back, but because at least it proved something was still alive between them.

Now, she's not so sure.

Love, on its own, no longer feels like enough. Not if it means carrying the weight of connection by herself. Not if it means wondering every day whether his silence is strength, or surrender. She can live without certainty. What she can't live without is truth, the kind that doesn't require decoding. The kind that says, I'm still here, and I'm choosing you, not just avoiding the worst of me.

Because she didn't fall in love with Jack for his restraint. She fell in love with the man who showed up anyway, even when he was raw and reckless and trying to hold everything together with trembling hands. She needs him to show up again. Not as a weapon. Not as a ghost. But as a partner. Or there won't be anything left to save.

The Misstep That Nearly Undoes It All

It wasn't a fight. That was the worst part.

There was no shouting, no slammed doors, no accusations flung like daggers across the room. Just a quiet, slow unraveling. The kind that doesn't register as a crisis until the damage is already done.

It started with something small, an offhand comment Lena made about Jack's tone during dinner with friends. He'd been distant, short with her, clearly irritated, though no one else seemed to notice. She waited until they got home, let him set his keys down, pour a glass of water, kick his shoes off. Then, gently, she said, "You seemed... off tonight. Like maybe you were mad at me?"

He didn't look up. "I wasn't mad."

She nodded, tried again. "It just felt like you were shutting me out. That kind of thing sticks with me, you know?"

Still nothing. Just a faint shrug and a quiet, "Okay."

The word landed like a locked door. No invitation. No curiosity. No Tell me what you mean. Just Okay. Like she'd delivered a complaint he had no intention of opening.

Lena felt her stomach knot. "Can we talk about it?" she asked, already knowing the answer. Jack's shoulders tightened almost imperceptibly. His eyes stayed on the glass in his hand. "There's nothing to talk about," he said.

That was the moment. The quiet, precise second when she felt herself drop through the floor.

Because it wasn't what he said, it was what he refused to say. What he refused to be. Present. Accountable. Engaged.

And she knew, in that breath, that he had checked out. Not in rage. Not in flight. But in refusal.

He didn't explode. He didn't escalate. He simply disappeared into the safest place he knew: withdrawal.

For the rest of the night, Jack barely spoke. He washed the dishes, turned off the lights, went to bed early. Lena stood in the hallway, stunned by the absence. It wasn't the absence of affection, she'd lived with that before. It was the absence of acknowledgment. Of shared reality. She had brought him her confusion, her fear, and he'd set it down beside him like clutter on a nightstand.

That night, she lay on her side of the bed, wide awake, staring into the dark and thinking about all the times Jack had insisted he was trying. That he was learning. That he wanted to be different. And she wondered, Is this the difference he meant? Because silence isn't change. Silence isn't growth. It's just a different version of the same need to avoid what makes him uncomfortable.

Later, when she brought it up again, days later, after the silence had curdled into resentment, Jack just shrugged.

No explanation. No ownership. Just a quick glance, a faint shoulder movement, and then back to whatever he was doing. Like it didn't matter. Like she didn't matter.

And that was the moment. Not when he shut down the first time, but now, when he chose not to revisit it. It wasn't because it was behind them, he never stepped into it in the first place.

Lena's take-away was this? *I don't want to deal with it. I don't want to deal with you.*

And underneath that: *Your feelings are more dangerous to me than my silence is to you.*

The rupture wasn't loud. It wasn't cinematic. But it was real. Because for Lena, it proved something she didn't want to admit, that even when Jack didn't lose control, she could still feel utterly alone with him. That even in the absence of harm, she was not safe. Because being unseen by the person you love, especially when you're finally brave enough to say what's true for you, is its own kind of injury.

Jack believed that restraint meant progress. That not reacting was proof of healing. But withholding, when done out of fear or avoidance, doesn't create safety. It creates ambiguity. Ambiguity, as research on relational trauma shows, is one of the most destabilizing dynamics for partners of emotionally unpredictable individuals (Freyd, 1996). It's not the volatility that wounds, it's the inconsistency. The emotional "now-you-see-me, now-you-don't" that makes you question your reality, your worth, your sanity.

Lena didn't want fireworks. She wanted presence. The Jack who used to fight her, even if poorly, at least still fought for the relationship. Now, he seemed to be playing dead. And while she understood the impulse, how deeply he feared losing control, she also recognized the power that silence gave him. Because when Jack shuts down, Lena has no handhold. No way in. No shared ground. And once again, it becomes her job to reestablish the connection, to figure out how to reach him without making it worse.

In that moment, the roles fully reversed. Once, Jack chased while Lena recoiled. Now, she was knocking on a door that refused to open. And the longer she stood there, the more she felt herself disappearing.

It's a common trauma response, this emotional stillness that masquerades as calm. According to Siegel (2012), individuals conditioned by early relational trauma often learn to survive through suppression. Their nervous systems equate stillness with safety. But in adult relationships, that survival strategy can function as a barrier to intimacy. What feels like protection to one partner feels like abandonment to the other.

Jack didn't mean to abandon her. He thought he was de-escalating. But he missed the point entirely.

Connection doesn't come from silence. It comes from risk. From staying in the room emotionally when things feel uncomfortable. From saying, I don't know what to say, but I'm listening. From letting yourself be wrong, be exposed, be human.

Jack didn't yell that night. But he also didn't choose her. And Lena, who has survived far worse, knows that sometimes the sharpest wounds are the ones that never draw blood.

Redefining Progress – Small Choices, Made Repeatedly

It happened in the kitchen. Not during an argument, not after some dramatic reveal, just an ordinary morning, thick with unspoken tension. The coffee pot had overflowed. Again. Jack had forgotten to empty the grounds from the day before, and now a sticky, bitter stream was seeping onto the counter, dripping onto the floor. Lena stood behind him, arms folded, already two hours into a rough day of her own. She didn't say anything at first. Just looked at the mess, then at him.

Jack could feel her gaze before she said a word. He braced himself.

She finally spoke, voice low. "Seriously? It takes two seconds."

It wasn't the words, it was the tone. Frustration clipped at the edges, disappointment under the surface. Familiar territory. The kind of comment that used to trigger something in him, a sense of being scolded, of being caught doing something wrong and humiliated for it. That internal voice would rise fast and hot: She thinks I'm careless. She thinks I'm a child. She's just like, No. He caught it.

Right there, standing in front of the ruined coffee pot, hand halfway to the paper towels, he caught it. The impulse to defend, to deflect, to say something sarcastic. To meet her tone with his own. To shut the conversation down before it could begin.

He swallowed it instead. Not perfectly, not gracefully. His jaw tightened, his breath hitched, but his voice stayed level.

"You know, for someone who claims not to be a morning person, you sure have a lot of opinions before 8 a.m."

He didn't look at her when he said it, but the corner of his mouth curled up almost imperceptibly into a tiny smile. Like he wasn't sure if it landed, but he knew it didn't explode. And for Jack, that was something. Maybe even enough.

And Lena, who had been preparing herself for the usual chain reaction, stood there blinking, disoriented by the flicker of humor. That wasn't avoidance. That was intention.

It wasn't a grand moment. Jack didn't turn and explain how he'd caught himself, didn't announce that this was a new version of him making better choices. But Lena saw it. She saw the effort in the small pause before his answer. The way he took the hit without striking back. The way he stayed in the room, in the moment, without trying to dominate it.

These are the things that don't show up in couple's therapy checklists or self-help bullet points. The invisible recalibrations. The split-second decision not to reach for a familiar weapon. The silence that doesn't signal retreat, but discipline.

For Lena, it marked a shift in her own perception. She had spent so long scanning for danger that she'd trained her body to flinch before anything even happened. Every misstep used to feel like a sign that nothing had changed, that she'd been foolish to stay, foolish to hope. But lately, she was beginning to notice the difference between patterns and perfection.

Because Jack still messed up. Still got defensive. Still slipped into old habits on occasion. But he also stopped himself more often. Circled back more quickly. Sat in discomfort longer without making her pay for it.

And Lena, for her part, began allowing space for the in-between. She stopped marking every slip as a failure. Stopped demanding proof of transformation in every conversation. She started watching for evidence of consistency instead, patterns, not performances. And the more she watched, the more she realized how many quiet repairs Jack was already making.

Trust, for them, was never going to be rebuilt in a single moment of breakthrough. It wasn't something Jack could earn with one apology or even one stretch of good behavior. It had to be layered, slowly, hesitantly, like stones across a river. Each one helping her believe that maybe this time, she wouldn't fall through.

They both still felt the weight of their past. That didn't vanish. But something else had started to grow alongside it, a kind of cautious partnership. Jack had begun to see that emotional regulation wasn't just about self-control. It was about showing up. Not just not harming her, but reaching for her. Taking responsibility without being cornered into it. Staying connected even when it felt safer to shut down.

This evolution mirrors what trauma recovery experts call the shift from "defensive non-engagement" to "vulnerable engagement" (Courtois & Ford, 2013). In this stage, individuals begin to recognize that true relational safety isn't about suppressing their emotions, but about choosing new ways to express them, ways that prioritize connection over self-protection.

Jack wasn't there yet. Not fully. But he was stepping into it. Because somewhere in the back of his mind, he'd started to understand that love couldn't survive in silence. That calming himself wasn't the same as being emotionally present. That keeping his hands to himself, his voice down, his feet planted in the room, these weren't just things she needed. They were things he needed too, if he wanted to build something real.

And Lena, watching him from across the room that morning, didn't say thank you. She didn't rush to affirm him, didn't turn the moment into a milestone. She just noticed. Filed it away. Let it be what it was: one small stone in a long, uneven path.

Because progress, she'd come to understand, doesn't look like he never did it again.

It looks like he saw it coming, and made a different choice.

The Cost of Fragile Hope

Lena stays. But not for the reasons she once clung to.

She no longer tells herself that love is enough. She doesn't romanticize their connection as fate, or believe that history guarantees a future. She doesn't point to his apologies like receipts of progress. What keeps her here is quieter now, more measured. It lives in the way he sometimes catches himself mid-sentence, breathes, and starts again. In the silence that doesn't feel like distance. In the moments where control doesn't follow tension, where the air stays still, and she stays standing.

People used to ask why she stayed. As if the answer could be summed up in one clean sentence. The real question was whether that love could evolve into something that didn't leave scars. Whether his remorse could finally mean something beyond the morning after.

She stayed because, underneath all the damage, there was still something worth watching. Because even after everything, she hadn't lost the cautious hope that he might learn how to love her without leaving scars.

She stays because he's trying again today. Not in grand declarations or sweeping gestures, but in small, often invisible recalibrations. He doesn't reach for dominance as often. He doesn't disappear as long. He doesn't rewrite reality to make himself more comfortable. Not every time. But sometimes.

Jack is not redeemed. He hasn't reached some final, polished version of himself. The past doesn't dissolve just because he no longer erupts. There are still days when he falls into silence, when his presence feels brittle, when Lena watches the old patterns ghost across his face like muscle memory. But there are also days, more of them now, when he interrupts those patterns. When he chooses presence over pride. When he asks instead of accuses.

That's the work. It's not glamorous. It doesn't guarantee anything. But it's real. And it costs him. She can see it in the way he flexes his hands when he's agitated, the way his jaw tightens when he's holding something in. Change, for Jack, is not natural. It's chosen. Re-chosen. Moment by moment.

And that's what Lena needs. Not guarantees. Not the illusion of peace. But evidence of a choice being made, not once, but repeatedly. Because trauma doesn't unwrite itself. And survival strategies don't vanish just because someone decides to do better. They wait. They whisper. They offer the familiar exit ramp the second discomfort shows up.

Real change is not the absence of failure, it's the presence of effort, even in the face of relapse.

Lena knows this now. She knows that even on the best days, their relationship sits on a frayed wire. The kind that no longer sparks, but still hums with tension underneath. And yet, she's seen what happens when that wire is handled gently. When it's inspected, rewired, reinforced one strand at a time.

She doesn't need to know that it will never break. She just needs to see him holding it in his hands, carefully, deliberately, every single day.

"I don't need certainty," she thinks. "I need to see him choose it, again, and again, and again."

PART IV: THE RESILIENT MARRIAGE – MAKING IT WORK (OR NOT)

DISCOVER THE REALITY OF WHAT COMES NEXT: A HARD-WON PLACE OF REBUILDING, OR A FINAL RELEASE. NO GUARANTEES, JUST THE GRIT OF DECISION.

Chapter Ten

Love and War – When a Relationship Is Worth Fighting For

There are moments in every high-conflict relationship where the fight doesn't come. The tension is there, the spark, the history, the weight of all the arguments that could erupt, but nothing ignites. No raised voices, no slammed doors. Just breath held a little too long. Eyes that don't meet. A silence that stretches into something unrecognizable.

For Jack and Lena, this was new territory. Not better. Just different. The absence of chaos didn't feel like peace. It felt like a missing pulse.

This chapter isn't about a breakthrough. It isn't about repair or even resolution. It's about what happens when both partners pull back from the edge but don't know how to step toward each other. Jack doesn't explode. Lena doesn't run.

But neither of them feels safe. Or seen. They're still inside the pattern, but it's quieter now, which makes the fear harder to name.

For Jack, this restraint feels like proof. For Lena, it feels like distance. And both of them, in their own way, are asking the same question: What now?

This is the space between survival and rebuilding. The place where effort exists without reward, and where presence is all that's left when trust has worn thin. It's not the answer. But it might be the beginning of one.

Jack's Remorse – Real, But Not Reliable

Jack sat on the edge of the bed, elbows on his knees, jaw flexing and unflexing like it had its own nervous system. The lamp across the room cast a soft yellow shadow, but he didn't move to turn it off. He could hear Lena in the other room, closing cabinets more firmly than necessary, the hush of footsteps deliberately not hurried. She was quiet, not avoiding him, but not inviting him either. And he hated how much worse that was than yelling.

They'd had an argument, if you could still call it that. It hadn't gone nuclear. He hadn't raised his voice. He hadn't punched the wall or slammed a door or grabbed her wrist when she tried to leave the conversation. He hadn't done any of it. That had to count for something.

Except it didn't feel like it did.

He thought he should feel proud, some part of him expected a ribbon or a thank-you or even a nod. Instead, there was this quiet. Heavy. Like she was waiting for something he hadn't done yet, even though all he could think was, I didn't lose it this time. That should've been the win. Right?

Jack's head dropped forward into his hands. I kept it together. I walked away. That had taken everything he had. He'd felt his chest tighten, rage scratching the back of his throat like a match that wouldn't strike. Her words had landed in a way that made his vision tunnel. Why do you always twist it around to be about you? she'd said.

And for a second, one long, pulsing second, he felt the world tilt. He hadn't even known what to say. His whole body had just gone tight and hot, and that thing, the part of him that kicked in when he felt cornered, had begun to stir. But he didn't let it rise. He walked into the other room. He took the exit.

And now? He sat alone in the dark, heart still pounding like he'd done something wrong anyway.

Shame, for Jack, was less of a weight and more of a fire escape. A burning room he had to get out of fast, before the smoke swallowed him. The longer he stayed in it, the more the walls closed in. He didn't sit in guilt. He sprinted from it, always looking for the cleanest window to throw himself through.

Because the longer he sat with what he'd done, what he might have done, the louder the voices got. The ones that said he'd never be different. That he wasn't better, just better-behaved. That restraint was nothing but a leash, and sooner or later, the chain would snap again.

He couldn't live in that space. So he reached for the closest lifeline: I didn't lose control. That counts for something. He said it to himself like a prayer. Like a protest.

In another room, Lena stood still in front of the sink, hands resting on the counter, eyes unfocused. She wasn't thinking about how Jack hadn't yelled. She was thinking about how close it had come.

She'd felt it, right there in his posture, in the way his hands flexed at his sides, in the sudden stillness that came right before he shut down. And for a moment, her body had braced for impact. Not because she thought he'd hit her this time. But because it felt familiar. Predictable. She didn't need violence to feel threatened. She just needed that airless space where her voice didn't matter, where his anger took over everything.

But it hadn't come. And she hadn't known what to do with that either.

Because if he didn't blow up, what was she supposed to do with all the adrenaline her body had already made? Where did the fear go when it had nowhere to land?

Jack's silence hadn't been comforting. It had been confusing. And the fact that he'd walked away, that he hadn't exploded, felt less like proof of progress and more like a tactical retreat. Not a transformation. A delay.

She hadn't thanked him. She wouldn't. *Why is not hurting me supposed to be impressive?* she thought, bitterly.

Jack didn't understand that his restraint wasn't visible from the outside. He expected credit for an effort that, to her, looked like nothing at all. No raised voice, no apology, no explanation, just silence and distance. She was tired of trying to read between the lines of his quiet.

In his mind, though, this was progress. Massive. Heroic. And the silence that followed it, the lack of affirmation or relief, gnawed at him in a way he couldn't name. His insides twisted into a question he didn't dare ask out loud: Why doesn't she see I'm trying?

Because she did see. That was the problem. She saw everything now. Not just the effort, but the pattern.

Freeze → Justify → Retreat → Expect Credit.

It wasn't a conscious strategy. It was reflex. He felt threatened, he tensed up. He didn't act out, but he withdrew instead, then came back later, subdued, hoping the absence of damage would be enough to patch things over.

But she'd caught on. The cycle was cleaner now, but it was still a cycle. And the more she noticed it, the less she could trust it.

Jack still thought of his worst moments as reactions, not decisions. The panic, the lashing out, the storms, they weren't choices, not to him. They were things that happened to him. Things that came over him like a seizure or a spell.

But Lena no longer saw it that way. She saw the micro-decisions: the moment he felt challenged, the moment he shut her out, the moment he flexed or flinched or fell silent. They weren't just symptoms, they were steps. Choices. And until he could see that, too, she knew this peace wouldn't hold.

He didn't see that his trigger was his responsibility. That being provoked wasn't the same as being possessed. That even if the rage rose like a wave, the board was still in his hand. He could choose to ride it, or not.

But that wasn't how Jack had been raised. Rage, to him, wasn't something you controlled. It was something that proved you were still alive. That you still mattered. That you hadn't gone soft. He'd been taught to fear weakness more than violence, to see control as a kind of emotional castration. Every time he held back, some part of him feared it made him invisible.

Which was exactly how Lena felt now. Invisible.

And that was the cruel irony neither of them had language for yet. His restraint, while hard-won, erased her reality. Her caution, while necessary, erased his effort. They were both swallowing words, hoping silence would translate into understanding. It didn't.

In that dim bedroom, Jack ran his hands over his face, heart still pounding with the residue of the argument that hadn't happened. He felt like a hero with no one to save. No one who noticed.

In the kitchen, Lena stood still, not out of peace but out of exhaustion. She wasn't waiting for him to erupt anymore. She was waiting to see if he would show up, really show up, or just disappear inside another quiet he expected her to interpret as growth.

Neither of them spoke. And that silence said everything.

Lena's Shift – From Comfort to Clarity

Lena no longer flinched when Jack apologized.

That wasn't the win it sounded like. Once, she would have read his remorse like a signal. The shakiness in his voice, the drop in his shoulders, the way he couldn't quite meet her eyes, those things seemed to mean something. They suggested she still mattered. That he hadn't lost her completely to whatever storm had overtaken him.

She used to think those moments were part of the repair. That maybe, just maybe, they were building something back in the aftermath. That each apology was a brick, fragile, maybe, but intentional.

But over time, she began to notice the rest of the pattern. The way remorse always came too easily, too soon. How it seemed less like a sign of change and more like a lifeline tossed out in panic, please don't leave me yet. It wasn't that Jack didn't mean it. He did. That was the hardest part. His regret was real. But real didn't mean reliable. Real didn't mean repair.

She'd begun to recognize that his apologies, while genuine, came wrapped in invisible terms: accept this, and don't make me stay in this shame too long. Comfort me, so I can feel better about what I did. Tell me I'm not the worst thing that's ever happened to you.

And for a while, she'd offered quiet space. Not comfort, space. She'd listened to his remorse, nodded, maybe stayed beside him longer than she wanted. It wasn't because she believed him. But because she hadn't yet decided not to.

But she's not that woman now. And she doesn't need his remorse to mean more than it does.

Lena had begun to detach, not from Jack, not entirely, but from the role she used to play in their recovery. The role of the emotional medic. The interpreter of storms. She wasn't racing toward the wreckage anymore. She was watching it from a safe distance, arms folded, measuring what he did when she didn't show up with gauze and forgiveness.

That shift didn't come all at once. It arrived in pieces, almost too small to notice. The first time she didn't respond to an apology with an obligatory hug. The night she didn't move toward him when his silence thickened with self-pity. The moment she saw him withdraw and chose not to close the gap.

It didn't feel cruel. It felt necessary. Her body still registered the pull to make things easier, for both of them. But eventually, clarity began to replace instinct. She started to see the machine at work, how every escalation was followed by despair, how every despair led to remorse, and how remorse too often reset the clock rather than dismantled the bomb.

Jack was remorseful. But he was also habitual. And she had been part of the habit.

She hadn't just tolerated the cycle. She'd studied it. In the early days, his remorse made her pause because it gave her something to measure. It suggested he still had skin in the game. That maybe there was more than reflex behind the regret. And for a while, that possibility bought time.

But not anymore.

These days, Lena doesn't test Jack by challenging him. She doesn't yell. She doesn't argue. She doesn't try to pin him down with questions or chase him out of his silence. She's tried all of that. And all it ever did was feed the loop, conflict, retreat, remorse, reset.

Now she tests him with stillness.

She doesn't slam doors. She doesn't run. She just... waits.

It drives Jack crazy.

He doesn't know what to do with the silence. He's always needed the conflict to feel engaged, even when he swore he hated it. He doesn't know how to read a Lena who won't rise to his bait, who won't engage, who won't feel with him in the same room.

He wants her mad. Yelling, crying, even leaving, that's something. That's interaction. That's proof she's still in it.

But Lena doesn't give him that anymore. She just goes still. Not as a punishment, but as a measurement.

Don't apologize, she thinks, sometimes saying it aloud now. Show me you're different when you're mad, not when you're sorry.

She's not even sure he hears her. Or if he does, if he understands what it means.

He still looks for the markers: Did I raise my voice? No? Then I'm improving.

Did I leave the room instead of exploding? That's growth. But Lena is watching something else entirely.

She's watching how he breathes when he feels criticized. How his jaw tightens when she disagrees. How quickly he switches from understanding to defensiveness. She's watching the subtle ways he still tries to control the narrative, even when he doesn't mean to. Even when he thinks he's being gentle.

And she's watching herself, too. How often she wants to step in, clarify, soothe. How often she fights the urge to explain herself just to keep things from spiraling. It's still a tug-of-war inside her, but she's getting better at letting go of the rope.

They've had entire evenings like this now. Nights where Jack sulks in the bedroom and Lena sits in the living room, unmoved. Not to provoke him. Not to ignore him. Just... waiting.

Not for his apology. For his consistency.

And he doesn't know how to give that yet. It's never been asked of him this way before. Not in silence. Not without prompting. Not without an emotional exchange to tether him to his own growth.

And that terrifies him more than he'll admit.

Because Lena isn't threatening to leave. She's not angry in the old way. She's not engaged. And Jack feels that shift in his bones. He feels the absence of her attention like a vacuum. Like a light switch flipped off in a room he doesn't know how to navigate anymore.

She's not disengaged. She's watching. And he doesn't know what she's waiting for.

That's the new discomfort in their silence. Not the looming threat of a blow-up, but the unbearable weight of evaluation. Lena isn't storming out. She's not crying. She's not laying down ultimatums.

She's studying him.

And it's not rage he sees in her eyes when they finally meet across the room, it's something colder. Not unkind, but resolute.

She's no longer invested in convincing him to change. She's invested in seeing if he will.

That shift, for Lena, was everything.

It wasn't that she stopped loving Jack. It was that she stopped mistaking emotional aftermath for progress. She stopped translating sincerity into change. She no longer gave apologies credit for work they hadn't done.

She doesn't want his promises. She wants his patterns to shift.

And until they do, she'll stay still. Not forever. But for now.

She's done performing forgiveness for the sake of peace. She's done softening the edges for a man who's still learning how not to swing between self-loathing and self-justification.

Jack thinks the silence means she's giving up. He doesn't understand yet: this stillness is her fight. It's her loudest demand.

It just doesn't sound like the kind he's used to hearing.

The Emotional Reversal – When Lena Pursues and Jack Retreats

It started with a question.

Not an accusation, not a trap. Just a question Lena had asked too many times in too many different ways. But this time, her tone didn't wobble. She didn't pad the edges. She didn't offer him a soft place to land.

"You want credit for not losing it?" Lena asked, voice steady.

Jack didn't answer right away. He stared at her like he hadn't heard. Like he needed a second to translate. His brow furrowed, his mouth opened slightly, then shut again. He looked toward the hallway, then back at her. She didn't blink.

"I didn't explode," he finally said. "That's something."

Lena didn't flinch. "That's a baseline, Jack. Not growth."

There it was. The shift. The air in the room changed, heavy with the weight of something unsaid but deeply felt. Lena was no longer the one retreating. She wasn't the one whispering assurances, smoothing over the jagged edge of his guilt. This time, she stood still and asked for proof.

And Jack, the man who once barreled through every emotional challenge like a battering ram, folded inward.

He turned away from her, not dramatically, not in anger. Just enough to create space. To breathe. He didn't know what to do with the demand in her voice, with the clarity. It was sharp, and it was clean, and it was terrifying because she was no longer confused.

That clarity stripped him bare.

He wanted to argue, he could feel the protest rising. You don't see what I'm holding back. You don't know how hard I'm trying. But something about the way she was looking at him made it impossible to speak. It wasn't disappointment in her eyes, she wasn't trying to hurt him. It was assessment. She was just... watching. Measuring.

And he hated how that made him feel.

Lena had always been the one who backed away when things got intense. The one who left the room, the house, the conversation. Her fear showed up in silence, in distance, in the sudden shift from openness to disappearance. Jack had learned to expect that rhythm, his explosion, her escape, the slow magnetic pull back toward each other.

But not tonight.

Tonight she was the one pressing forward. Not in rage, but in resolve. She needed answers. She needed evidence. And that shift, that need, made Jack want to disappear.

He didn't recognize himself in that moment. Or her.

He felt cornered, even though she hadn't raised her voice. He felt judged, even though she hadn't accused him of anything. And that feeling, being emotionally exposed, with no clear script to follow, was worse than a fight.

Jack's instinct was to shut down.

He moved toward the window, arms crossed, posture stiff. He wasn't leaving, but he wasn't staying either. Not in the way she needed. And Lena felt that wall go up like a door closing in her face.

It enraged her in a way that surprised even her.

Because this was what he said he wanted. A real conversation. A moment where she stayed, calmly, and told him what she needed without threats or tears. And now that she was doing it, now that she was giving him the very thing he'd claimed to crave, he was backing out of it.

"Say something," she pressed. "Don't just stand there."

Jack's hands clenched and opened, the same nervous rhythm she'd come to recognize. His jaw tightened. But still, he said nothing.

And Lena felt the wave of heat rise in her chest. Not the kind that led to screaming. The kind that wanted to shake the truth out of him.

"I'm not asking about what you avoided," she said, her voice low, controlled, dangerous in its precision. "I'm asking what you're doing different in the moment. Because this, this quiet, this freezing, isn't it."

"I'm trying," Jack said finally. "I didn't lose control."

"You keep saying that like it's impressive."

"It is," he shot back, turning toward her now, defensive edge creeping in. "You don't know how close I was."

"And you don't know how close I was to leaving," she said. "Again."

Silence.

Jack's breath caught in his throat. Lena didn't flinch.

"I know you're trying," she said, softer now, but not retreating. "But trying isn't changing. Not yet."

He looked at her like she'd hit him. Not because it wasn't true, but because it was.

Lena didn't soften. Not this time. Because she wasn't angry. She was awake.

Jack had always feared judgment. Even when he said he wanted feedback, what he really wanted was reassurance. He wanted to be told he was better, that he was improving, that the past didn't count against him. And Lena, for years, had given him that. She'd buffered his shame with compassion, translated his outbursts into trauma language, treated his regret as repentance.

But now she wanted something more than regret.

She wanted accountability. Not the kind you confess once and then file away, but the kind you live with. The kind that changes how you move. How you speak. How you react in the moment, not in the aftermath.

And Jack couldn't give her that. Not yet. Because he didn't know how to hold shame without drowning in it. He still thought being confronted meant being condemned. He still confused exposure with humiliation. So when Lena pressed in, not emotionally, but intellectually, he panicked.

He shut down to preserve himself.

But Lena saw it now for what it was. Not arrogance. Not manipulation. Fear.

He was terrified of being seen and found lacking. Of being told he was still the same man she once fled from. And in that fear, he didn't explode, he disappeared.

Meanwhile, Lena wasn't running. She wasn't even trembling. She stood firm, eyes clear, voice steady, asking not for penance, but for proof.

And that was the reversal neither of them had prepared for.

Jack was fragile now, emotionally raw, hunted by ghosts of his own making. And Lena, the one who used to collapse under emotional pressure, was steady. Strong. Sharp in her questions, clear in her demands. But underneath all that poise, she was scared too.

Because she needed this to be real. She needed this to be more than a temporary calm. She needed to believe that the man standing in front of her could not only stop himself, but see himself, really see what he was doing, not just what he was avoiding.

She was chasing certainty because she couldn't afford to be wrong again.

And Jack was avoiding confrontation because he couldn't afford to hear that he still wasn't enough.

They were both afraid. Just not of each other. Of themselves.

The room stayed quiet a little too long.

"I'm trying," Jack said again, quieter now. "You don't think I'm trying?"

Lena's eyes softened, just slightly. "I think you're trying not to mess up. That's not the same as healing."

Jack looked down.

"I don't want to lose you."

"Then stop trying not to fail," she said. "Start showing me you actually get what matters to me."

There it was. The ask beneath the anger. The plea beneath the pressure.

And Jack, for once, didn't argue. He just stood there, breathing. Still hiding. But not leaving.

Not yet.

The Crisis of Almost – The Fight That Didn't Happen

Jack could feel it building, the heat behind his eyes, the tingling in his fingers, the familiar rush of blood to his ears that made everything sound underwater. Lena was standing too close. Not physically, but emotionally. Her words had been calm, but pointed. There was nowhere to dodge, no sarcasm to deflect with, no retreat that didn't look like cowardice.

He hated this part. The edge.

The moment before the storm, when his body surged with the need to do something, slam a door, yell, pace, anything to dispel the pressure coiling in his chest. His jaw tightened reflexively. Then his hands, clenched at his sides, started their rhythm: clench, open, clench again. Not fists, never fists, but the motion of someone trying to hold on to something slippery. His own restraint.

Lena didn't raise her voice. She didn't threaten. She just stood there, asking the kind of questions that made his skin crawl. What does remorse mean if nothing changes? How many times do we survive this cycle before we stop calling it survival?

Jack's breath grew short. His vision narrowed. His shoulders stiffened. Every instinct screamed at him to move, to react, to push back. To do anything but stay in this raw, wordless moment where he couldn't win and couldn't explain.

But he didn't explode.

He walked out.

Not in a huff. Not with the dramatic punctuation of slamming doors or tossed objects. He just turned, quietly, and left the room. One foot in front of the other, like walking away was something he practiced. But it wasn't muscle memory, it was war. Inside, every part of him howled with resistance. Leaving without lashing out felt like bleeding without screaming.

He went to the back porch. The cold bit at his skin the second he opened the door. That helped. The shock of it. He stood there, hands on the railing, air slicing into his lungs, and tried to slow his breathing.

This is what you wanted, he told himself. To break the pattern. To get out before it gets bad.

He closed his eyes. His jaw ached from clenching. His hands wouldn't stay still. He flexed them again, slower this time, measured, like that small act might keep something worse from breaking loose.

And for the first time in a long time, he didn't feel victorious for walking away. He felt sick.

Because back in the house, Lena was still standing in the hallway, staring at the space he'd just vacated.

And what she felt wasn't relief. Not quite.

More like the moment after an echo fades, when the room feels too quiet and you're not sure what you were hoping to hear. She had braced for the blowout, had steeled herself for the same explosion she'd come to know so well. But it didn't come. Jack didn't raise his voice. He didn't unravel. He left.

She should have felt safe. Protected. Maybe even proud of him. But instead, she felt hollow.

Wasn't this what she'd begged for all those years? For him to not fight back? For him to choose pause over fury? To walk away before things turned violent or cruel?

So why did it feel so weird?

The question haunted her even as she turned toward the couch, sat down, and folded her arms across her chest to sit with this for a moment. The room was too quiet. No footsteps, no yelling, no sound of a slammed door echoing up the stairs. Just absence.

Was the fight the tether? The proof they were still in it?

She wasn't sure. But the silence didn't feel like peace, not yet. It felt unfamiliar. Like distance trying on a new costume. Not cold. Just... hollow.

Lena didn't miss the yelling. She didn't miss the slammed doors or sharp exits. But at least in those moments, she knew exactly what was happening. This quiet? This low, clean exit?

She wasn't sure what to make of it. Not because it hurt. But because it didn't.

She pressed her palm to her chest, as if to ground herself, to feel her own pulse still thudding beneath the surface. She didn't want him to fail. She didn't want him to explode. But she hadn't expected him to just disappear, either.

She wasn't grieving the absence of conflict. She was adjusting to it. There was no storm to clean up after. No harsh words to weigh or translate. No apology waiting in the wings.

Just stillness.

And in that stillness, Lena felt something settle, not peace exactly, but space. A quiet without warning signs. A calm she hadn't had to earn.

It wasn't comforting. But it wasn't threatening either.

It was new. And she wasn't sure yet what to do with that.

Jack stood outside for twenty minutes before he came back in. He didn't expect a welcome. He didn't expect a conversation. He just moved past her on the couch, silent, and disappeared into the bedroom. She didn't follow.

They slept back to back that night. Not angry. Not cold. Just... unsure.

Because neither of them knew what this meant yet.

Jack had done the thing they'd both hoped he would do, he'd pulled out before escalation. He'd chosen silence over shouting, distance over destruction. But he hadn't offered comfort afterward. He hadn't returned with reflection, or with remorse, or even with curiosity.

He had simply stopped the fight.

And Lena, who had long believed that ending the cycle would feel like healing, was now confronted with something harder: the grief of peace without connection.

This new quiet, though safer, felt lonelier than any argument they'd ever had.

Because there was no engagement, no spark, no evidence of emotional life between them. Just a truce built on exhaustion.

Neither of them was sure if this was progress or withdrawal.

Neither of them knew if the pattern was breaking, or just going quiet long enough to change shape.

And that ambiguity, that almost, was harder than any explosion.

When Love Isn't Enough, But It's Not Nothing

Jack stood in the doorway like someone who wasn't sure he belonged in the room.

It had been two days since the fight that didn't happen. Two days of short phrases and long silences, of passing each other like strangers in their own kitchen. No shouting, no door slamming, no cries for closeness. Just quiet. Dense and unyielding.

Lena sat on the couch, one leg tucked under her, elbow braced on the armrest, fingers drumming lightly against her jaw. Still. Not withdrawn, just lost in her thoughts. She didn't look up when he entered. But she didn't leave either.

He cleared his throat. She didn't flinch. That was something.

Jack leaned against the wall. Not too close, not too far. He looked like he was waiting for permission to speak. And then, without buildup, without defense or performance, he asked the one thing he'd never said out loud before.

"What do I do," he said, voice low and unsure, "when I'm not enough?"

Lena's breath caught. Not because it was manipulative, there was no edge in his tone, no desperation. Just honest confusion. Honest fear.

She didn't answer right away. Her gaze stayed fixed on the blanket in her lap. There was a part of her that wanted to offer something, comfort, reassurance, even just words to fill the space. But she was learning to sit in silence too. To let discomfort do its work.

Because she didn't know the answer.

She'd asked herself the same thing, in different words. What do I do when love isn't enough? When the person in front of me is trying, but I'm still so guarded. When the damage isn't fresh anymore, but it still echoes in every silence. When I want to believe, but I don't want to be fooled again.

They were both on the edge of surrender. Just not to the same outcome.

Jack wasn't raging, but he wasn't sure how to stay. Lena wasn't leaving, but she wasn't sure how to hope.

The line between them wasn't thick with conflict anymore. It was thin. Fragile. And that made it even more dangerous.

It would take so little to tear it, so little to give up. A shrug. A silence too long. A gesture too sharp. Or, worst of all, nothing at all.

He stepped forward, just enough to sit on the edge of the armchair across from her. He didn't try to close the gap between them. He just sat, elbows on his knees, hands loose between them. The clenching and flexing had stopped. He looked tired in a way Lena had never seen before, like something inside him had gone still.

She looked up.

"You think not yelling is enough," she said quietly. "You think walking out instead of blowing up proves something. And maybe it does. But it's not the thing I need."

He nodded slowly. "Then what is?"

She hesitated. Not because she didn't have an answer, but because she had too many. And none of them felt solid yet. They were still forming, still unraveling from the version of herself who used to measure safety in volume, and love in whatever came after the damage.

"I don't know," she said. "Not yet."

Jack exhaled and looked down. Not in defeat. Just in acknowledgement.

For the first time, Lena felt like he wasn't trying to sell her anything. Not his pain, not his progress. He was just... there. Present.

It was a strange kind of intimacy. This quiet where no one was performing. No one was fixing. Just two people sitting with the ache of their own limits.

Lena wasn't packed to leave. But she had, emotionally, zipped the suitcase. Not out of threat. Out of reality. She couldn't keep doing this forever. Couldn't keep circling the same drain, hoping next time it would feel like a bath.

But she wasn't gone.

Jack wasn't raging. But he was unraveling. The old tools didn't work anymore. Fury, withdrawal, remorse, they no longer moved her. They didn't even move him. He wasn't sure who he was without them. But here he was anyway.

Not enough. But still here.

And in a relationship like theirs, maybe that was what passed for hope.

Not trust. Not repair. Not belief in a bright, new chapter. Just this.

The choosing to stay in the room. To ask hard questions. To sit through the uncertainty. To not turn away from the look in her eyes that said, I don't know if I can do this much longer.

There was something sacred in that tension. Something unsentimental but real. The kind of love that had nothing to do with fairy tales and everything to do with stamina.

They weren't better. They weren't safe. But they were still trying to understand what trying meant.

Jack leaned back, hands resting on his thighs. He didn't ask for forgiveness. Didn't list his efforts. He just watched her, face open, waiting for something she couldn't give him yet. But maybe someday.

Lena uncrossed her legs slowly, set her feet on the floor, and leaned forward with her elbows on her knees, mirroring him without thinking.

"You keep asking what to do," she said. "I think maybe the answer isn't something to do. Maybe it's something to become."

Jack nodded again, slowly. She could see the words landing, not bouncing off.

And that was all. There was no big moment. No kiss. No confession. Just the steady hum of proximity. The weight of two people sitting in the same silence without trying to break it.

It wasn't resolution.

But it wasn't nothing.

The Space Between the Storms

Sometimes the hardest part of growth is that it doesn't feel like progress. It feels like absence. Like silence where there used to be shouting. Like distance where there used to be fire. Jack didn't rage, and Lena didn't flee, but what remained between them was quieter, heavier, and far more uncertain.

This chapter wasn't about redemption. It wasn't about breakthroughs or sweeping change. It was about what happens just before that, when both partners step back from the familiar chaos and don't yet know how to replace it with connection. Jack's remorse is real, but incomplete. Lena's stillness isn't withdrawal; it's data collection. And in the absence of explosions, the fear becomes harder to name.

Here, we see what survival looks like after the storm, the moment when two people sit across from each other with no script left. Jack doesn't know how to show up differently yet, only how to hold back. Lena isn't sure whether staying is strength or denial. They haven't rebuilt anything. But they haven't left either.

And in relationships like theirs, that's where hope lives, not in the certainty of healing, but in the refusal to look away.

Reflection: "What Do I Do When I'm Not Enough?"

This is Jack's question, but it belongs to both partners in a high-conflict relationship.

If you are the one trying to change, ask yourself:
- What do I expect to receive in exchange for my effort, validation, forgiveness, relief?
- Am I measuring progress by what I avoid rather than how I engage?
- Can I hold space for my partner's doubt without needing to be rescued from it?

If you are the one watching and waiting:
- Do I confuse calm with connection?
- Have I equated remorse with repair?
- What would it take for me to feel emotionally safe again, and have I named it?

Write your answers down, but don't aim to solve them today. Some questions aren't meant to be answered quickly. They're meant to be lived inside, until clarity grows where confusion once ruled.

Chapter Eleven

The Art of Repair – What Happens After the Battle

The Moment After Survival

They weren't touching. That was new.

Not in a standoff way, not in the deliberate silence of two people waiting to see who flinches first. It was quieter than that. Stranger, even. Jack sat across from Lena, one arm draped across the back of the couch like he'd forgotten it was there. His hand stayed still, no idle flexing of fingers or compulsive rubbing at his jaw, just stillness. Lena hadn't spoken in ten minutes, maybe more. But she hadn't left, either. Her legs were pulled up beside her, not in retreat, but in self-containment. Everything about her posture said: I'm not running. But I'm not stepping in until I know it's safe.

That safety, whatever remained of it, now depended on what they didn't say next.

They'd fought the night before. No slammed doors, no shattered glass, not this time. This was the kind of fight where truths spilled out so sharp and unfiltered that they left emotional bruises, echoes of things both of them swore they'd never say again, or never admit to in the first place. It was the kind of fight where clarity arrives like wreckage. And now, here they were: still together, technically. Not broken up, not repaired. Just... here.

Neither of them reached for the other. Neither filled the silence with hopeful platitudes or tired promises. Maybe that was the first sign of growth. Or maybe it was just fatigue.

Lena exhaled, more sigh than breath, the kind that tried to release pressure but came out as steam. Jack didn't react. She noticed that, too.

In the past, he would've jumped in to soothe the air between them. Or defend it. Or reset it somehow, start talking about groceries or the next day's schedule, like emotional detonation could be swept under a calendar. But now he just sat, breathing slow, gaze unfixed. Not numb. Not absent. Just... cautious. Like someone who finally understands that his words have weight, and that using them carelessly might shatter what's left of the floor beneath him.

Lena's mind felt like a hallway with too many locked doors. She didn't want to open any of them yet. Not because she was afraid of what she'd find, but because she already knew. She'd been in every room in this house before. Shame. Hope.

Fury. Despair. The temptation to rewrite. The temptation to burn it all down. The only new room, if it existed, was the one they'd have to build together. And right now, neither of them had reached for the blueprint.

She looked at him then. Not searching his face for guilt, or softness, or the version of him she'd once used to justify staying. Just looking. Taking inventory. Was he still the man who had made her feel like her feelings shouldn't exist when he was angry? The one who made her small with dismissive silence and volcanic certainty? Or was he something else now, something in between what he'd been and what he might become?

Jack met her eyes and held them.

That moment, muted and brittle, felt more honest than a thousand apologies.

"I keep thinking," he said finally, voice quiet, "if we're still sitting here… then I don't know. Maybe it's not over. Maybe it means something."

Lena didn't answer. Not yet. She waited, watching. That tone, that cautious offering, was new. Not performative. Not fishing. He wasn't asking her to fill in the meaning. He was voicing a question he hadn't figured out how to finish.

"I mean," he tried again, "we've been through worse, haven't we?"

There it was. Familiar ground. The tilt toward minimizing, even if he didn't mean to. The framing of survival as progress.

She didn't pounce on it, didn't snap back. She just blinked slowly and said, "Have we?"

Jack winced, not dramatically, but it landed. His eyes dropped for a second, then came back up.

"I don't know," he admitted. "It just... it feels like if we're still sitting here, not hating each other, not done, then maybe we've figured something out."

Lena cocked her head. "Or maybe we're just used to crawling out of the wreckage."

He nodded once, jaw flexing. "Yeah. Could be that too."

That was the thing with them. They were always at risk of measuring progress by proximity. If they hadn't walked away, if they were still talking, if they hadn't crossed a new line lately, then maybe they were improving. Maybe staying meant healing. But even that metric was suspect. Staying had cost Lena pieces of herself she hadn't noticed were gone until she tried to use them again.

Still. She hadn't left. Not after last night. Not after the conversation that stripped both of them to emotional scaffolding. And Jack hadn't stormed out, hadn't twisted her silence into something he could weaponize, hadn't tried to outrun the discomfort. That was something.

He didn't try to defend what he'd said, or didn't say. He just looked at her, quiet, jaw tight, and finally said, "I just want to be happy. I want us to be happy."

It wasn't naïve. It wasn't even hopeful. It was desperate in that soft, worn-out way Jack had when his armor finally gave out.

Lena didn't flinch. Didn't offer him anything more than the truth she had left.

"Yeah."

It wasn't sarcastic. It wasn't kind. It just was.

Because she wanted that too. She just wasn't sure there was still room for that kind of happiness in what they'd become.

Jack looked at her, brow furrowed.

"We burned things down before, and tried to fix it. Even pretended we were okay afterwards. This time? I'm not pretending, and here we are. So now what?"

Jack didn't answer. He knew better than to answer too quickly.

The silence returned, but it wasn't hostile. It was cautious. Reverent, even.

She studied him again. Not the man she wanted him to be. Not the man he claimed to be. Just the one in front of her, quiet, no longer defensive, finally aware that control had never protected them. It had only delayed the fallout.

Trust was not going to bloom from this silence. But maybe clarity could.

What were they, if not what they've been?

That was the unspoken question between them. It hovered there, daring them both to look at each other without the stories they'd used as scaffolding.

Not lovers clawing their way back to passion. Not enemies licking their wounds. Not trauma-bonded messes trying to outrun the latest emotional explosion.

Just two people, finally out of the fog, asking themselves the only question that mattered now:

If we don't want to go back... then what the hell do we build instead?

Lena's Demand for Unfiltered Truth

The silence didn't last.

It held just long enough to suggest a new kind of tension, one that wasn't primed to explode, but might erode instead. Lena shifted her position, letting her feet slide to the floor. She didn't square off, didn't posture. Just sat up, grounded. She'd learned over time that it wasn't confrontation that rattled Jack, it was calm honesty, delivered without the preamble of apology or threat.

"I need to say something," she said, tone neutral.

Jack's head tilted slightly. Not a nod, not an invitation. Just awareness. He was bracing, but not defensive. Not yet.

"You do this thing," she continued, "after we fight. After something bad happens."

His gaze dropped, and she saw the flicker of tension ripple across his jaw. There it was. The preparation. The part of him that began mentally sorting through the night before, not to reflect, but to strategize.

"You rewrite it," she said.

His head snapped up.

"I don't mean you lie. Not outright. But you do reframe it, like I'm making up some fantasy. You say things like, 'You don't believe that,' and suddenly I'm not allowed to just... hold the truth. My truth."

Jack didn't hesitate. "You don't believe that."

The silence that followed was eerily quiet. He heard it the second it left his mouth.

Lena didn't flinch. Didn't argue. Just let it sit there, like a truth he'd tripped over and handed back to her.

He exhaled, slow. "Shit."

No excuses. No spin. Not this time.

She still didn't speak.

Jack ran a hand down his face. "I wasn't trying to twist it. I just... but if I don't say what's going on in my head, then I'm just the bad guy in your story."

"And maybe you were," Lena said, calm. "For that moment."

He flinched. But not like before.

He didn't jump to defend himself. Didn't throw the usual lines, You kept pushing. You cornered me. You know what I'm like when you start screaming at me.

They were there. Right there. Just under the surface, clawing for air. But this time, they stayed put.

The defenses rose, but they didn't launch. They hung in his jaw, in the tension behind his eyes, visible, unspoken.

And for once, he didn't ask her to pretend they weren't there.

"Every time you start trying to reframe it, it feels like you're trying to make me lose my grip on what I know actually happened. That's gaslighting."

Jack frowned. "You think I'm gaslighting you?"

"Yes," she said gently. "And you're gaslighting yourself."

He looked away then, the way he always did when shame crowded the room. Hands clenched once, then relaxed. He didn't get up. Didn't storm out or start pacing. But the energy shifted, tighter now, more fragile.

Lena waited.

"I'm not trying to twist your words," he said finally. "That's not what I'm doing."

"That may not be your intent," she said. "But gaslighting is making someone question their reality until they can't trust what they saw or felt. And when you say it out loud, directed at me, you hear it yourself, and rewrite things so you don't have to sit in what actually happened."

Jack took a breath. "I snapped. I know I did. I'm not proud of it. But if you didn't make me snap, then what did? I can't control it. It just happens."

"You can control it," Lena said. "And you have. I've seen you do it."

She didn't raise her voice. She didn't have to.

"It's a choice. One you make when the stakes are high enough."

"Last night," she said, voice steady, "you raised your voice and started towards me like you were going to tackle me. I backed up to the wall. You didn't touch me. But you stood over me, hands against the wall behind my head, and I froze. In that moment, I was scared of you. And you? You were just 'making a point.' And then, when I asked you to back away from me, you just stood there, flexing your jaw with your face right in mine, staring at me like I was your enemy."

Jack opened his eyes again, wrestling with defensive justification and disbelief, but guilt bleeding through.

"That happened," Lena continued. "That's what I experienced. You don't get to tell me I don't believe that, or that's not what happened, or there was nothing wrong with what happened, or even that you didn't mean to scare me."

"I'm not saying that didn't happen. I just, if I don't say what was going on with me, then I might as well not even exist. Why am I even here if all I am to you is a threat?"

"You're not a threat to me," Lena said. "You're a man I love, who sometimes becomes unsafe. That's the truth I live with. And it's the truth you have to sit with, too."

He flinched again, more deeply this time, but stayed. That was something.

"That's not who I am," he said.

"I know," Lena replied. "But that's still who you were to me last night."

Silence again.

Jack's voice, when it came again, was raw. "Here's what I remember."

"We were talking, and you started backing away from me," he said. "I needed you to listen to me. I knew you were cornered, and I kept going. I didn't touch you, but I did stop you from leaving."

Lena didn't reply. Didn't nod. She just listened.

"I didn't mean to scare you," he added reflexively.

She tilted her head. "Seriously?"

He shut his mouth. Let the words settle.

"I remember the look on your face," he said. "I remember thinking, Why is she acting like I'm dangerous? I'm not even yelling. But I knew. Deep down. I knew I was pushing it. I just... I couldn't let it go. I needed you to listen to me."

"And you needed me to be afraid, so I would."

Jack winced.

"That's the part you never say," she whispered. "That sometimes scaring me works. And that's why it happens again."

It was the ugliest truth. And the most sacred.

Jack's head dropped into his hands. Not dramatically. Not theatrically. Just tired.

"That's probably true," he murmured. "I need some time to think on that."

"Sure," she said.

He stayed like that for a while, bent, quiet, not asking for anything. No reassurance. No absolution. Just stillness again. But not the brittle kind. The raw kind. The kind that says, I'm finally sitting in the wreckage, and I'm not pretending it's a construction site.

Lena exhaled deeply. This, this moment right here, was the closest they'd ever come to real repair. Not because it felt good. But because it certainly didn't. Because Jack wasn't hiding behind context or tone or the softness of his regret. He was owning what she'd lived through, without asking her to water it down.

He didn't try to touch her. Didn't ask if they were okay. He just sat there, truth heavy between them, and let it be what it was.

Finally.

Naming What Was Lost

Lena hadn't planned to say it. It wasn't a line she'd rehearsed or a speech she'd tucked into the back pocket of a thousand past arguments, waiting for the right moment to throw it down like a final verdict. It came up quiet. Unrushed. The way truth sometimes does when it's no longer afraid of being dismissed.

"I wasn't just afraid," she said.

Jack looked up, startled. He'd been tracing the worn seam of his jeans with a single fingertip, stuck in some halfway space between guilt and stillness. His eyes met hers quickly, too quickly, and she saw it flash through him, the bracing. The subtle tension that crept in when he knew something important was about to be said, and he wasn't sure whether to lean in or shut down.

Lena didn't flinch. "You didn't just scare me," she continued, voice low and steady. "You made me feel like the only way to survive you was to disappear."

Jack blinked once. No recoil, no sharp intake of breath. But everything in his posture stiffened, shoulders pulled in, chin dipped, hands now still.

She wasn't trying to hurt him. That was the thing. She'd long since learned that trying to punish Jack only triggered more defensiveness, more rewriting. This wasn't about payback. This was about finally putting words to something she had never said out loud, not because she hadn't known it, but because she hadn't believed she was allowed to name it for what it truly was.

She never called it fear. That word felt too misplaced. Fear was something you could point to. She called it strength, protecting herself. Putting up a wall. Fear wasn't even on her radar, because if it was fear, it meant she wasn't strong. It meant she was vulnerable, smaller than she needed to be. And she couldn't afford that. She wasn't trying to disappear, but this felt like the only safe option. And the worst part? It worked.

Jack opened his mouth, reflexively, and she saw the sentence forming: *If you weren't so...*

But he didn't finish it.

His jaw tightened. His mouth closed again. And for the first time in a long time, he didn't rush in with the usual defense.

Lena nodded slightly, recognizing the restraint. That, in itself, was progress.

"You stood over me, blocked me in, and just kept going. Like the louder and closer you got, the more I'd finally listen. Sure, I set you off, but once it started, I wasn't your wife anymore. I could've been anyone or anything standing in front of you for you to unload on."

She was calm. Not cold. But emotionally precise. It was the kind of calm Jack had once mistaken for detachment, before he understood it was the calm of a woman making sure she didn't disappear again.

"I wanted you to hear me," he said quietly. "I *needed* you to hear me."

She nodded. "I know. But you didn't stop to notice that I had already checked out. You just pushed harder."

Jack swallowed. His fingers moved again, slow, searching for rhythm, for regulation.

"I thought if I stopped talking, you wouldn't hear me," he said.

"You weren't trying to make me hear you," she replied. "You were trying to win."

That wasn't cruelty. That was clarity. Jack sat with it.

He didn't like how that sounded when she said it out loud. But he couldn't argue with it. Yeah, he pushed. She froze. That wasn't misunderstanding. That was control.

And it worked.

So he said nothing.

Lena didn't soften. She didn't say, I know you didn't mean it. She didn't offer a graceful exit. That was the old pattern. She'd speak up. He'd offer a solution. She'd see he felt bad. And that was the end of it, until the next time. And the truth would get buried under good intentions.

Not this time.

"Do you know what it costs to stay with someone who makes you feel like you don't exist?" Lena asked.

Jack nodded. Then shook his head. "Yeah," he said quietly. "I do."

Lena blinked. That answer surprised her, until he added: "That's how I feel when you shut down. Like nothing I say matters."

She didn't argue. Didn't soften.

But she didn't look away.

"Yeah," she said quietly. "I know that feeling too."

She studied him. He wasn't hiding, but he was unraveling. Quietly. He looked like a man trying to keep from splitting apart under the pressure of finally seeing himself as she had seen him. Not as a villain. Not as a monster. But as someone who, however unintentionally, had made love feel like submission.

"I wasn't trying to shut you down," he said eventually.

"But you wanted me silent," she replied.

He winced. "Only when I felt like I was losing it."

"And that's what you have to own."

He nodded. Still not running. But visibly rattled.

This, this was the reversal. Lena, once the one who folded, who retreated into cool distance when things got heavy, now stood her ground. She didn't withdraw. She held the line.

Jack, the man who used to steer away the second things got too real, now sat through the discomfort. He didn't defend himself. He didn't turn it into a monologue. He didn't ask for forgiveness.

But he stayed quiet, jaw tight, hands still. He finally realized that she saw him, exactly as he was. No rationalizations. No buffering. Just the raw truth: *I didn't lay a hand on you. I didn't yell at you. But I did corner you. And you froze. And I didn't stop.*

He looked at her, eyes unguarded now.

"I'm listening," he said.

Lena didn't thank him. She just nodded. As if to say: *You should be.*

They stayed there for a long moment, each silently rearranging their understanding of what had been lost.

Lena hadn't just lost trust. She'd lost voice, size, shape. And now she was reclaiming it, not through rage or abandonment, but through naming. Through staying and still saying the hard thing.

Jack hadn't just lost control. He'd lost the illusion that good intentions make harm less real. That being sorry meant he could steer how she remembers it. That pain, if explained well enough, could be forgiven before it's truly understood.

He hadn't said it yet, not fully, but Lena could feel it coming. Not the apology. The reckoning.

She wasn't here for his regret. She was here for the day he stopped needing her forgiveness more than he needed to carry the truth with her.

When Repair Isn't Reassurance

Jack didn't speak for a long time. The words sat just behind his teeth, ready but unsure, like a half-drawn breath he wasn't sure he was allowed to take. Lena hadn't moved since the last thing she'd said, and he wasn't sure if her stillness meant he was safe to speak... or if she was done listening altogether.

So when he finally asked, it came low and level. No desperation. No theatrics. Just a question suspended in the space between uncertainty and a kind of quiet courage.

"What do you want from me?"

Not a plea. Not a trap. Just a man, stripped of all his practiced lines, unsure if there was anything left she was willing to reach for.

Lena turned to look at him fully, her gaze sharp but not cruel. He saw her measure the question, turn it over, see if it came with strings.

It didn't.

She exhaled through her nose, slow and steady, like the answer itself wasn't simple enough to live in one sentence. And it wasn't.

"I want you," she said finally, "to stop needing me to be okay with what wasn't."

Jack's mouth twitched, just barely. Not a smile. Not a grimace. Something in between. He nodded once, but didn't speak.

"I want you," she continued, "to stop thinking everything's fine just because I let it go"

That one landed harder. His jaw tightened, and the skin beneath his eyes pulled taut like he was trying not to wince. But he didn't interrupt.

"And I want you to let me be angry," she said, "without you spiraling or making it all about you."

Jack swallowed hard. He looked down for a moment, palms pressed together like he was holding something fragile between them, an apology he wasn't sure she needed, or wanted, or would even recognize as different this time.

"I'm not asking you to fix anything," Lena said. "That's part of the problem. You keep thinking this is a problem to be fixed. Like if you say the right words, or used just the right apology, it resets the clock. Like we can pretend none of it ever happened."

He didn't look up. But she knew he heard every syllable.

"I don't want repair that applies just another coat of paint," she said. "I want repair that strips off all the old and applies something new, fresh, and maybe even wonderful."

Jack closed his eyes.

A tear slipped down Jack's cheek, trailing fast down the side of his nose before he could catch it. He didn't brush it away. For the first time, he understood why Lena hadn't trusted him with her softness.

And that hurt. He thought he was her protector. He thought his strength was her safety net. But in truth? He was the reason she had to stay armored.

Now, she wasn't reaching back. And he wasn't collapsing.

Something new was happening. Not comfortable. Not comforting. But true.

"I didn't get it," Jack said, voice rough. "I thought I was fixing things, I was just trying to get us past the mess fast enough to forget it happened."

Lena didn't say anything at first. Then: "You weren't fixing. You were controlling the damage."

Jack's jaw tightened, but he didn't argue.

"You wanted to look better," she said, "not be better."

He nodded. Once. It was all he could manage.

"I thought if I could explain it right, make you understand where I was coming from, you'd be happy," he muttered.

"No," Lena said. "You thought if you said it right, I'd stop looking at you like you were the problem."

That one hit. Harder than she expected. But he didn't flinch. Not this time.

Jack didn't say anything at first. Just stared at the floor like he was trying to track the weight of what she'd just said.

When he finally spoke, it was low. "So what now?"

Lena didn't answer right away. Then: "That depends on what you do when I stop catching the blowback from your worst moments."

That landed. But he didn't flinch. Didn't fire back. He just nodded. Slowly. Like he was still deciding whether he could carry that kind of weight.

They sat there, not quite side by side. Not reaching for anything. Just not leaving.

There was no fix. No grand reset. Just Jack, staying in it. And Lena, not having to shrink to make room for him.

It wasn't closure. But maybe it was the start of something neither of them had trusted before.

Something that didn't rush.

Choosing With Eyes Wide Open

The light outside had shifted by the time either of them spoke again.

It wasn't quite sunset yet, but the quality of it had changed, that early, honey-colored slant that turns everything soft around the edges, whether it deserves softness or not. It filtered through the window in long, golden streaks, brushing the floor and the table and the two of them sitting not quite together, not quite apart.

Lena leaned back slightly, exhaling like someone who'd been carrying too much for too long and finally set it down. Her shoulders were no less tense, but they weren't braced anymore. There was space now. Not safety. Not clarity. But space.

Jack rested his elbows on his knees, hands clasped, head low. He wasn't crumbling. But he was cracked open in a way that felt... honest. For once, there was nothing in him trying to steer this into comfort. Nothing angling for her reassurance. He had no idea what she was going to say next, and for the first time in a long time, he didn't feel entitled to it.

Lena crossed her arms, eyes fixed on the floor.

"If we stay," she said, "it can't be because we're scared to leave."

Jack said nothing.

"It has to be because we know exactly who and what we're staying with. And we stay anyway."

Jack gave a slow nod. Nothing certain in it. Just quiet agreement.

"So what do you know?" she asked.

He didn't look at her right away.

"I know I want us, even knowing what it's been," he said.

A pause.

"I still want to be happy, I want *you* to be happy."

Another pause. Then, quieter: "I know I messed things up, and I know 'sorry' doesn't fix it."

Lena didn't answer. Not yet.

And Jack didn't try to fill the silence.

Lena inhaled, slow and steady. "I didn't come into this trusting. I've always held people at a distance. You just gave me more reasons to keep doing it."

"That's fair," he said.

They let that hang there. No protest. No performance. No urge to disprove each other's limits.

"We're not healed.," Jack said, voice quieter now, "But maybe we're not lying to ourselves anymore."

Lena's head tilted slightly. "Or each other," she echoed. "I'll take that over promises any day."

He looked at her then, really looked. And it hit him, this was the most intimate they'd been in months. No touching. No declarations. Just two people not hiding.

"I won't expect you to act like it never happened," he said. "Not anymore."

Lena's eyes didn't soften. But something behind them did.

"Then maybe," she said, "I'll stop acting like I don't care about you, or us. Sometimes."

A long pause followed. But it didn't ache. It settled.

That was the thing no one tells you about surviving each other: sometimes the hardest part isn't deciding whether to stay or go. It's learning to look at the person across from you, not as the one who hurt you, or saved you, or disappointed you, but as someone who's just as scarred and scared and still trying.

Jack didn't promise he'd never raise his voice again. Lena didn't swear she'd never pull away. But for the first time, they both stopped asking each other to be someone else.

And that, oddly, felt like relief.

Outside, a breeze moved the curtains. Jack sat back, hands open now, not clenched. Lena uncrossed her legs and stretched them out in front of her. They didn't move closer. But they didn't move apart, either.

No final decision. No breakthrough. Just presence.

They had no idea what tomorrow looked like. But for the first time, neither of them needed to rush toward it to escape today.

They were here. They knew what they were. What they weren't. And what they might, just maybe, still be.

Letting the Truth Sit Between You

Repair is not forgiveness.

It's not the warm wash of reconciliation or the soothing balm of mutual absolution. It's colder than that. Harder. Quieter. It's two people standing on either side of the truth, not rewriting it, not minimizing it, not using love as a shortcut around it, and deciding, in that raw clarity, to stay. Not because the pain has passed, but because the truth matters more than comfort.

Forgiveness may come later. Or it may not. But repair begins the moment both people stop trying to win the argument and start listening for the wound.

For high-conflict couples, especially those shaped by trauma or conditioned volatility, the aftermath of rupture can be more destabilizing than the rupture itself. There's no script for what happens after the adrenaline wears off and the silence sets in. There's just this: a choice to keep showing up, not to forget, but to remember together.

And that remembering has weight.

It means letting go of the need to be the one who was "right." It means allowing your partner's experience to exist without defense. It means giving up the idea that repair is a reset button, and accepting instead that it's a step, one that doesn't always look like progress.

Sometimes repair sounds like: I hear you, even if I hate what I did.

Sometimes it sounds like: I'm still angry, and I still care.

Sometimes it sounds like nothing at all, because silence is no longer a weapon, it's a truce.

For those still navigating this terrain, here's the question:

What conversations have you avoided because you fear they'll confirm what you already know?

What truths are you afraid to name, not because they're unbearable, but because they might change everything? Or worse, because they might not?

This chapter wasn't about redemption. It was about recognition. And the tiniest shift that comes when you stop trying to rewrite the past and start letting it live in the room with you, breathing, uncomfortable, unedited, and still reach across it.

They didn't hug it out. They didn't walk off into the sunset.

They just didn't walk away.

And maybe, for now, that was enough.

Chapter Twelve

Unstoppable, Immovable, and Still Standing

When Everything Could Go Sideways

Jack didn't even look up when he said it. That was the first sign.

"It's not that hard to put the damn lid on," he muttered, voice low but deliberate, like he was already halfway through the argument in his head.

Lena froze mid-step in the hallway, her hand wrapped around a fresh towel from the dryer. The bathroom light was still on behind her. The laundry basket still sat at her feet. And the toothpaste cap, apparently the day's harbinger of doom, lay exactly where she'd left it.

She didn't respond. Not at first. Just that tiny inhale, audible only to her. But her shoulders had already gone up. Her spine had already straightened.

Jack noticed that part. He always did.

He looked over then, eyes narrowed, not in rage, not yet, but in that assessing, anticipatory way. Like he was deciding whether to commit to the coming war or let the moment pass. His fingers drummed twice against the kitchen counter. Then curled into his palm.

"This again?" Lena said finally, towel still dangling at her side. The words came out flat, too slow. Controlled.

He turned toward her. Not fast, not confrontational. But it was enough to make her instinct kick. Her feet wanted to step back.

They didn't.

Jack's eyes flicked to the hallway, to the counter, to the cap, and back to her.

"No. Not 'this again.' Just... it's not new, Lena. It's every day."

There it was. The pivot. His voice had softened, but the edge sharpened. That careful blend of weary and accusatory that always made her feel like she'd forgotten something vital and done it on purpose.

Her brain did the math before her mouth could form words. If she snapped, he'd dig in. If she walked off, he'd follow, convinced she didn't care. If she turned it into a joke, he'd call her dismissive.

She did none of those things.

"I heard you," she said. And she stayed still.

Jack blinked. Just once. Then his jaw did that thing, it tightened, loosened. Like he was biting down on a response and chewing it twice before swallowing.

The silence sat between them, bloated and twitchy. Waiting.

"I wasn't trying to start anything," he said, eventually.

She didn't say then why did you? even though it sat neatly at the top of her tongue.

"I know," she answered instead.

And that was new. That was the shift. Neither of them fully understood it yet, but something had cracked in the script. A line had gone missing, and neither of them rushed to improvise.

Jack stepped away from the counter, not storming, not gesturing, just... walking. Slow enough not to seem aggressive, direct enough not to be retreat. He passed her in the hallway, close enough that she could feel the body heat off his arm, but not so close it felt like a dare.

She didn't flinch. That was new too.

He stopped just past her, back still turned.

"I'm just tired of feeling like I don't matter in the little ways," he said, more to the hallway than to her. "That's all."

She could have fired back. Could have listed every time he'd ignored her discomfort or talked over her or steamrolled a boundary in the name of "just talking." But she didn't. Not because she was conceding. Because in that moment, she saw the thread.

Jack wasn't mad about the toothpaste. He just needed to feel like he mattered.

Lena wasn't being difficult. She needed to know she still had a choice.

Lena reached down, picked up the cap, and twisted it on. No sarcasm. No theatrics. Just motion. And then she walked past him, back toward the bathroom.

She didn't slam the door.

He didn't throw anything.

No one declared victory. No one waved a white flag.

But when Lena turned on the faucet to wash her face, her hands weren't shaking. And Jack didn't leave the house.

It wasn't peace. It was restraint. It was both of them standing at the edge of the old cycle and, for once, not jumping.

It was not the ending of a pattern. But it was the first moment they both chose not to reenact it. And maybe that meant something.

Maybe, for now, it was enough.

When Control Isn't Power

Jack stood in the doorway of the spare room, arms crossed, one hand gripping the opposite elbow, the way he did when he wasn't sure if he was holding himself up or holding himself back. The room wasn't much, just a half-unpacked box of winter clothes, a folding chair draped with a sweatshirt, and a half-wilted plant Lena had rescued from the clearance shelf at Lowe's. But for the last hour, it had been his retreat. Not in the dramatic sense, no doors slammed, no threats tossed behind him. He'd just needed space. From her. From himself.

His mind kept circling the same thought like a dog wearing out the grass in the yard: You didn't lose it. This time, you didn't lose it.

But the quiet didn't feel triumphant. It felt... unstable. Like he'd shoved a boulder back into place, but knew the slope would eventually win.

He grabbed the folding chair, popped it open and sat down, leaning forward, elbows on his knees. He looked down at his hands. They weren't shaking, exactly, but his fingers kept opening and closing, like he hadn't quite convinced his body the moment was over.

He knew what it looked like from the outside, how the toothpaste thing would seem petty, ridiculous. He'd tried telling himself that, too. It's just a cap, Jack. Just plastic and mint and forgetfulness. But he also knew what it felt like. Like being ignored. Like being left behind. Like the quiet buildup before the door slammed shut and never opened again.

That wasn't Lena's fault. But his brain didn't always care whose fault it was.

He hated this part. The thinking afterward. The mental autopsy. The way every conflict made him relive moments he'd never fully understood to begin with.

He remembered something from a few days earlier. A dumb argument about groceries, he couldn't even recall the spark. Just the flash. Lena had said something offhanded. He'd taken it as a slight. And before he knew it, he was raising his voice. Not yelling. Not yet. But looming. Fast. The kind of tone that said back down or I'll make you. Her face had changed instantly, and he'd felt it before he understood it.

He'd stopped talking. Mid-sentence. Mouth still half-open, breath still climbing. He remembered walking out. Not because he was the bigger person, but because he saw it in her eyes, the way she'd gone still. Not scared, just done. Like she was already planning her exit. And somehow, that felt worse than if she'd screamed at him.

She hadn't followed him.

And he hadn't gone back in the room. Not for almost an hour.

That had shaken him more than the argument itself. Because somewhere deep in the part of his brain that couldn't afford to be vulnerable, the old pressure kicked in: You're losing the grip here. She's not reacting. You don't know where this is going, and that's the problem. He felt a pressure rising in him. An urgency. Like if he didn't steer it back into something he could control, anger, argument, anything, he'd end up on the outside of it, watching everything slip past him without a say.

It wasn't about her leaving. It was about not being able to stop it. That was what hollowed him out, the moment he realized he might not have the leverage anymore.

And for a breath or two, that scared him.

Not because he needed to win, but because he didn't know who he was without the fight.

She saw the good in him. Not blindly, not always. But enough. And if she ever stopped, if all she saw was threat, weight, damage, he wasn't sure what would be left.

He'd always thought control was strength. That if he held everything tight enough, his temper, the room, her, he could stop the worst from happening. But that wasn't strength. That was fear, dressed up like authority.

Control looked like power. But underneath it was panic. The kind he never learned how to name. The kind that showed up as pressure in his chest, a shortness in his breath, a tightening in his jaw. The kind that told him: Don't get soft. Don't lose your edge. Don't let anyone see you bleed.

Staying in control meant no one could humiliate him again. It was how he stayed one step ahead of that feeling, like the kid with a backpack and no ride, watching everyone else get picked up first. It was how he stopped being the one left holding the fallout when everyone else walked away.

But it didn't keep people close. It just made them careful. And careful wasn't love.

That was the part he was still trying to get right.

Because when things felt good, when Lena laughed at something dumb he said, or gave him that look that didn't mean I'm tolerating you, but I like being around you, his chest would clench with something almost like awe. Like he'd tricked the system and gotten something he wasn't supposed to have.

But the second her tone shifted, or her back turned, or she missed something that mattered to him, it was like falling through a trapdoor. Suddenly, he was back in the void. Unseen. Unheard. Easy to leave.

And people who could be left didn't get to matter.

So he'd reach. And press. And escalate. Not to punish, but to prove. To anchor himself in the moment. To stay relevant.

He buried his face in his hands, exhaling hard. *I don't want to lose her, but if I hold tighter, I will.*

He'd thought saying it would make it easier. It didn't.

But something had shifted. Not just that he didn't explode, but that he chose not to.

He hadn't walked out to punish her. He walked out because he knew what staying in that room would've cost.

That had to count for something. Right?

The question echoed back at him like most of them did, quietly, without answer.

Jack stood and walked back to the doorway. He could hear Lena moving in the kitchen. Not loudly. Not cautiously. Just... existing. That was all. And he felt his breath settle a little.

Maybe this was what change looked like, not triumph, not calm, but hesitation. Just enough pause to make a different choice. Just enough presence to resist the old pull.

He wasn't steady yet. He didn't know if he ever would be. But he was learning what steady looked like.

It looked like letting someone walk away without following.

It looked like listening without needing to win.

It looked like not having the last word.

It looked like leaving the toothpaste cap alone.

Staying Isn't Giving In

Lena sat on the edge of the tub, the overhead light humming with that low fluorescent whine she always meant to fix. Her face was still damp from the washcloth, skin pinked at the edges like she'd scrubbed off more than just the day. She stared at the towel in her lap, twisting the corner into a tight coil.

This was the kind of moment she used to run from.

Not because it was loud or violent or even dramatic. But because it was familiar. The quiet tension. The almost-fight. The way Jack's frustration landed in the space between them like a dropped suitcase, heavy, abrupt, expectant. He never said pick this up for me, but she always felt like she had to. That was the trap. Not yelling. Not threats. Expectations.

And that was what cornered her, not his words, but the invisible consequence of not meeting them.

She used to run because she'd learned to. Because disengaging had always been the only way to stay whole. Because pushing back, claiming space, insisting on her right to not explain, those had never been safe options growing up. She didn't come from a home where disagreement meant debate. It meant distance. Her opinions were "attitude." Her silence was "defiance." Her body had learned early that autonomy came at a price. Affection was conditional. Approval was currency. And withholding was the weapon of choice.

So she adapted. She learned how to read a room before she entered it. Learned how to soften her tone, calculate her phrasing, anticipate the shift in someone else's mood before they noticed it themselves. She knew how to disappear without leaving. How to make herself small enough to avoid consequences.

But it wasn't just about survival. It was about not betraying the version of herself others needed her to be. Obedient. Agreeable. Manageable.

The worst part wasn't losing her voice, it was how often she willingly gave it up.

That part took longer to admit.

And for years, that pattern followed her into every relationship she touched. It wasn't that she couldn't argue, she could. God, she could. But the moment she felt cornered, emotionally backed into a place where nothing she said would land without consequence, she'd vanish. Not always physically. Sometimes just mentally. She'd go blank inside. Shut down. Disappear beneath the surface like a diver running out of air.

With Jack, it had been harder. Because he didn't let her just disappear, he needed her engaged. Needed the fight, the reaction, the tether. And when she pulled back, he pursued harder. The more she disengaged, the more he pushed. And eventually, she'd snap. Not because she wanted to, but because the pressure built to a breaking point. And then she would become the volatile one.

That's what no one understood. That's what her friends missed when they asked why she didn't just leave. They didn't see the whiplash. The fact that it wasn't always Jack who escalated first. Sometimes it was her. Sometimes she was the one who couldn't let it go, who pushed the issue, who needed the resolution now. Because silence felt like suffocation. Because not being heard felt like erasure.

But this time... she hadn't run. Not emotionally. Not mentally. Not physically.

She'd stayed in the room. Sat with the discomfort. Let his words come, and then let them go.

That was new.

That was hers.

She could still feel the prickle of resistance in her spine, the urge to bolt, to retreat behind a locked door and breathe herself back into equilibrium. But she hadn't done that. She'd looked at him, responded without flinching, and held her ground without escalating.

She wasn't staying because he asked her to.

She wasn't staying because she owed him the benefit of the doubt.

She wasn't staying because she'd been guilted or worn down or pacified by softness.

She was staying because she chose to.

That was the difference. That was what changed the air around her.

She could leave. Anytime. That had become her quiet mantra over the last year. I can leave. I'm not stuck. I'm not trapped. And oddly, knowing she could go made it easier to stay.

She looked at her reflection in the mirror. No bravado. Just her. Still here.

"Staying isn't giving in," she whispered to herself, the words so soft the mirror didn't even fog.

It was something her last counselor had said, one of the few phrases that stuck. Back then, she hadn't really understood what it meant. She'd spent years overexplaining herself to keep the peace. And if that didn't work and someone couldn't handle a boundary, she didn't argue, she just left. If it made them uncomfortable, that was their problem.

But not this time.

Jack hadn't punished her for not backing down. He hadn't raised his voice, hadn't pressed closer, hadn't pulled out the old familiar guilt trips. He'd paused. Looked uncertain. Even backed off.

It wasn't perfection, but it was space. And she hadn't had to demand it.

She thought about the night months ago, the worst of it. The one that broke something in both of them. She'd fled then, body on fire, nerves screaming, every cell in her body recoiling from the way his hands had closed around her wrists. He hadn't hurt her, not exactly. But that wasn't the point. He'd held her. And she hadn't consented. And he knew that. He knew.

She had walked out that night certain she'd never return.

But she had. Returning wasn't the easy option, but the decision was hers to make.

And ever since, she'd had to rebuild what "staying" meant. It wasn't resignation. It wasn't compliance. It was a choice made with her whole body, not out of fear, but out of clarity.

Tonight, she'd chosen not to walk. She needed to know she could, without compromising herself.

That was autonomy.

That was what survival had never given her: the space to decide.

And tomorrow? She didn't know. Maybe they'd fight again. Maybe the old patterns would creep back in, slick and persuasive. But this moment was hers. This breath. This decision.

She picked up the damp towel, hung it with more care than usual, and stepped out into the hallway, not armored, not defensive, but whole.

Jack wasn't in sight. She heard the faint sound of dishes clinking in the sink. A small thing. A human thing.

She didn't smile. Not quite. But something in her chest loosened. Not in surrender. In permission.

She had stayed.

And not because she had to.

Because she wanted to.

Not Fixed, Not Broken, Just A Choice

Jack found her in the hallway, arms crossed but at ease, back against the wall near the thermostat. She looked up when he stepped around the corner but didn't move. Neither did he.

For a second, the silence stretched with a sense of uncertainty.

He rubbed the back of his neck. "I almost said something I'd regret."

Lena didn't nod or speak right away. Just watched him. Measured the pause.

Jack shifted his weight. "Earlier. With the toothpaste. It was stupid. But I felt it coming." His voice thinned for a second, like it didn't want to carry the rest of the sentence. "That burn in the back of my throat, the one that says raise your voice or lose the moment. I caught it just before it broke loose."

Lena let her arms drop. "I know," she said. "I saw it."

That surprised him. Not that she noticed, she always noticed, but that she wasn't flinching from it. She was just saying it plain. No edge. No hidden message.

He walked a little closer, then leaned a shoulder against the opposite wall, folding his arms. The hallway was narrow enough that their feet nearly touched.

"I didn't want to win," he said. "Not really. But somewhere in my head, it felt like if I let it go, I'd be dismissed. Like…if I didn't fight to be heard, I'd be ignored like I wasn't even here."

Lena nodded slowly, eyes still on his. "I get that."

He exhaled. "I thought I had to be right. Or louder. Or just… the one who didn't back down. I didn't know I could just be here and not lose."

That landed between them like something sacred. Not a confession. Not a plea. Just truth, raw and uneven.

Lena glanced down, then back up again. "I almost walked," she said.

He tensed, then caught himself. Didn't react. Didn't ask why. Just waited.

"It's what I do when I feel boxed in," she continued. "Because when I think the next words out of your mouth are going to push me back into some version of myself I don't want to be again."

Jack didn't look away. "What stopped you?"

She smiled. Not soft. Wry. "I realized I didn't have to run to have space. That I could stay and still hold my ground."

He tilted his head. "That's new."

"It is," she agreed. "For both of us."

They stood like that a while. Not dramatic. Not distant. Just... there. Two people in a hallway, neither storming off, neither demanding closure.

Jack looked toward the living room. "It's weird," he said. "There's this instinct to wrap it all up in a nice bow. Say something perfect so we can call this a breakthrough."

Lena snorted. "Yeah, that's not happening."

"I know," he said, smiling faintly. "But still."

She stepped off the wall, brushing past him with a gentleness that felt deliberate. She headed toward the kitchen, and he followed.

There was nothing ceremonial about the way they moved. No dramatic soundtrack. No moment of clarity that erased all the others. Just two people stacking dishes into the dishwasher, moving around each other without commentary.

When Lena finally spoke again, it was over the running faucet.

"I used to think walking away meant power," she said. "Turns out, staying with my eyes open is harder."

Jack didn't respond right away. He reached into the sink, handed her the last plate.

"I used to think raising my voice meant I was still in the room," he said quietly. "Turns out, listening takes more strength than shouting ever did."

She met his eyes then. And for a long second, neither of them blinked.

There were no declarations. No apologies. Just presence.

And that, somehow, felt bigger than either.

Lena dried her hands on the edge of the towel and leaned against the counter. Jack mirrored her on the opposite side. They weren't touching. But the space between them didn't feel loaded this time. It just felt like breath.

"I'm not promising I won't screw up again," he said.

"I'm not promising I'll always stay," she replied.

They both nodded.

But neither left.

Sometimes, that's all there is. A pause in the storm. A silence that doesn't mean danger. A moment when two people, who've hurt each other more than they care to admit, choose not to draw blood again.

They hadn't solved anything.

They just didn't want to lose the ground they'd finally gained.

They didn't need to be fixed.

They weren't broken.

They were just choosing.

And for tonight, that was enough.

Still Standing

The sun had dipped just low enough to pull gold from the edge of the sky, the kind of light that made the porch look warmer than it actually was. Jack sat on the top step, elbows resting on his knees, a chipped mug of lukewarm coffee in his hand. Lena had dragged a blanket around her shoulders, feet tucked beneath her in the old patio chair. It creaked when she shifted, but neither of them acknowledged it. The silence was steady. Not thick. Not waiting for the next thing. Just... there.

They'd eaten together. Nothing fancy, leftover chili and half-stale cornbread, the last slice buttered just the way he liked it. She hadn't said a word when she handed him the plate, and he hadn't tried to over-thank her. The ease between them was fragile, but it held.

At some point, Jack had brought out the laundry basket, and they'd folded shirts on the couch, stacking them in sloppy towers without commentary. One of his undershirts ended up in her pile, and she didn't toss it back.

Now, out here, the air smelled faintly like someone nearby had a fire pit going. Lena watched a small trail of smoke curl up past the neighbor's fence and disappear into the darkening sky.

"You want the last blanket?" she asked.

Jack looked over, shook his head. "Nah. You always steal it anyway."

She raised an eyebrow. "It's not stealing if I claim it before you get attached."

He chuckled, and it came out real. No defensiveness. No guarded tone. Just a laugh that landed between them like a small, shared secret.

She let it sit, then added, "Besides, you hog the bed. Blanket's the least I can take."

He looked like he might argue, then caught himself. Held up both hands in mock surrender. "Okay. You win."

She blinked, surprised by the ease of it. Not the words, he'd said them before. But the tone. There was no bite in it this time. No smirk that said you're still wrong. Just a quiet release.

Something flickered between them then. It wasn't a moment, exactly. More like an exhale. Like they'd both remembered they were allowed to be gentle.

Lena leaned back, eyes tracing the shadowed lines of the porch railing.

They weren't healed.

They weren't fixed.

Some nights would still unravel. Some fights would still come out sideways. She knew that. So did he.

But they were here. Folding laundry. Arguing about blankets. Laughing, a little.

She watched Jack tip his head back to look at the sky. His profile was softer in this light, less drawn. And when he caught her looking, he didn't flinch or look away.

Instead, he held her gaze, and in that silent exchange was the smallest, truest acknowledgment.

We survived this one.

She turned her face back toward the horizon and pulled the blanket tighter around her shoulders.

We're not healed. We're not safe from it. But we're here. And right now, that's enough.

The Small Things That Hold

The cabinet door had been hanging crooked for weeks.

It wasn't a big deal, not enough to start a fight over, not enough to justify calling it urgent. Just a hinge that creaked too loudly and sagged an inch lower than the others. Lena had stopped noticing it. Jack hadn't.

He crouched on the tile floor, screwdriver in hand, a replacement hinge beside him. He'd found it in the junk drawer where everything from extra screws to expired batteries lived. No one asked him to fix it. There was no speech about doing better, no performative chore list. Just a quiet Sunday morning and the weight of small intentions.

Lena watched from the hallway, one socked foot resting on the baseboard. She didn't interrupt. She liked watching him like this, head down, jaw tight in concentration, trying to get something right that no one else had demanded he fix.

He'd already replaced the stripped screws, repositioned the frame, and wiped off the smudged fingerprints on the cabinet door. She didn't comment. He didn't look up.

When he finally stood and opened the door, smoothly, silently, there was a flicker of satisfaction across his face. Not pride. Not "look what I did." Just a private moment of this matters, even if no one sees it.

He put the screwdriver away, washed his hands, and moved on to something else. As if it hadn't been an act of repair at all.

But Lena saw it.

Not just the hinge. Not just the fix.

She saw the choice.

The quiet effort. The deliberate care. The decision to put something back in place, It wasn't broken enough to ruin everything, but it mattered in the long run.

This wasn't a happy ending. It wasn't an ending at all.

It was a man fixing something he once would've ignored. A woman noticing without needing to narrate it. A hinge that now swung straight.

Unstoppable. Immovable.

And still standing.

Keeping the Fight Honest

Because Truth Is How We Stay in the Game

Now that you've seen what real love looks like when it's messy, raw, and full of resistance... you know you're not alone.

You've got the stories. The insights. The tools. You've seen what it takes to stay, or to leave, with eyes wide open.

But for someone else still in the thick of it, still wondering *"Is it just me?"*, your voice could be the hand that pulls them out of the fog.

By leaving an honest review of this book on Amazon, you help other people in high-conflict relationships find clarity, comfort, and maybe even courage.

Your review says:

You're not crazy.

You're not alone.

This might not fix everything, but it will make you feel seen.

This book lives because people like you keep it alive. Every shared story, every honest word, it all matters.

https://www.amazon.com/review/review-your-purchases/?asin=B0F6MJK1RY

Thank you for helping us keep the truth on the table.

With gratitude,

Renae C. Linde

Conclusion: The Strength in Resistance

Every relationship tells a story, and not all love stories are written in soft whispers and seamless harmony. Some are etched in fire, sharpened by conflict, and forged through the constant push and pull of strong-willed souls who refuse to yield, yet refuse to walk away. This book has explored the nature of **high-friction relationships**, the kind that thrive not despite resistance, but because of it.

What We've Learned

Across these twelve chapters, we have seen that love, at its core, is not about erasing differences but about **understanding how they shape us**. The lessons are clear:
- **Attachment styles influence how we connect, fight, and reconcile.** Knowing whether we lean

anxious, avoidant, or secure allows us to navigate conflict with greater clarity.

- **Engagement-seeking behavior is often misunderstood.** Some partners push buttons, not out of malice, but as a desperate bid for connection.

- **Boundaries are not abandonment, and space is not rejection.** A healthy relationship requires both closeness and independence in careful balance.

- **Power struggles are less about control and more about feeling heard.** Learning to differentiate between destructive battles and necessary tension is key.

- **Emotional triggers dictate how we react to conflict.** Becoming aware of them allows us to break cycles of automatic, damaging responses.

- **Conflict is not the enemy. Stagnation is.** The goal is not to eliminate disagreement but to engage with it in ways that strengthen the bond rather than weaken it.

- **Repair matters more than resolution.** Some fights will never be neatly tied up, but every emotional wound must be addressed if the relationship is to thrive.

Love That Endures

Jack and Lena's story is one of persistence. They didn't seek a love that was effortless, they sought a love that was worth the effort. Their relationship was not about avoiding friction, but about **learning how to navigate it without losing themselves or each other.**

A marriage built on resistance is not for everyone. It is demanding. It requires endurance. But for those who choose it, it is **deeply fulfilling**. It keeps love alive, engagement high, and passion burning long after others have faded into complacency.

If you find yourself in a relationship like this, know that your love does not have to be quiet to be true. It does not have to be easy to be real. **It simply has to be chosen, every day, by both of you.**

In the end, the most important lesson is this: **Love is not about who wins. Love is about who stays in the fight.**

References

American Psychiatric Association. (2013). Diagnostic and statistical manual of mental disorders (5th ed.). Arlington, VA: American Psychiatric Publishing.

Arriaga, X. B., Kumashiro, M., Finkel, E. J., & VanderDrift, L. E. (2014). The social-cognitive dynamics of relationship initiation, maintenance, and repair. In J. A. Simpson & L. Campbell (Eds.), The Oxford handbook of close relationships (pp. 169–194). Oxford University Press.

Ashton, M. C., Lee, K., & Paunonen, S. V. (2002). What is the central feature of extraversion? Social attention versus reward sensitivity. Journal of Personality and Social Psychology, 83(1), 245–251. https://doi.org/10.1037/0022-3514.83.1.245

Baxter, L. A., & Montgomery, B. M. (1996). Relating: Dialogues and dialectics. Guilford Press.

Bowlby, J. (1988). A secure base: Parent-child attachment and healthy human development. Basic Books.

Briere, J., & Scott, C. (2015). Principles of trauma therapy: A guide to symptoms, evaluation, and treatment (2nd ed.). Sage Publications.

Brown, B. (2012). Daring greatly: How the courage to be vulnerable transforms the way we live, love, parent, and lead. Gotham Books.

Brown, B. (2018). Dare to lead: Brave work. Tough conversations. Whole hearts. Random House.

Carnes, P. (1997). The betrayal bond: Breaking free of exploitive relationships. Health Communications.

Cassidy, J., & Berlin, L. J. (1994). The insecure/ambivalent pattern of attachment: Theory and research. Child Development, 65(4), 971–991. https://doi.org/10.2307/1131298

Caughlin, J. P., & Huston, T. L. (2006). The affective structure of marriage. Journal of Marriage and Family, 68(2), 376–394.

Christensen, A., & Heavey, C. L. (1990). Gender and conflict structure in marital interaction: A demand/withdraw analysis. Journal of Personality and Social Psychology, 59(1), 73–81.

Coan, J. A., Schaefer, H. S., & Davidson, R. J. (2006). Lending a hand: Social regulation of the neural response to threat. Psychological Science, 17(12), 1032–1039.

Courtois, C. A., & Ford, J. D. (2013). Treatment of complex trauma: A sequenced, relationship-based approach. Guilford Press.

Courtois, C. A., & Ford, J. D. (2016). Treating complex traumatic stress disorders in adults: Scientific foundations and therapeutic models. Guilford Publications.

Cummings, E. M., & Davies, P. T. (2010). Marital conflict and children: An emotional security perspective. Guilford Press.

Davidson, R. J., & Begley, S. (2012). The emotional life of your brain. Hudson Street Press.

Fincham, F. D., & Beach, S. R. H. (2010). Marriage in the new millennium: A decade in review. Journal of Marriage and Family, 72(3), 630–649. https://doi.org/10.1111/j.1741-37 37.2010.00722.x

Firestone, L. (2012). The self under siege: A therapeutic model for differentiating from destructive thoughts and behaviors. Routledge.

Fisher, H. (2004). Why we love: The nature and chemistry of romantic love. Henry Holt & Co.

Fisher, J. (2017). Healing the fragmented selves of trauma survivors: Overcoming internal self-alienation. Routledge.

Fisher, J., & Ogden, P. (2015). Sensorimotor psychotherapy: Interventions for trauma and attachment. W. W. Norton & Company.

Ford, J. D., & Courtois, C. A. (2013). Treating complex traumatic stress disorders in adults: Scientific foundations and therapeutic models. Guilford Press.

Ford, J. D., & Courtois, C. A. (2014). Treating complex traumatic stress disorders in adults: Scientific foundations and therapeutic models. Guilford Press.

Freyd, J. J. (1996). Betrayal trauma: The logic of forgetting childhood abuse. Harvard University Press.

Gao, G. (2008). Communication, trust, and interpersonal harmony: A comparison of Japanese, Korean, and Chinese cultures. Asian Journal of Communication, 18(3), 245–259. https://doi.org/10.1080/01292980802207062

Goleman, D. (1995). Emotional intelligence: Why it can matter more than IQ. Bantam Books.

Gottman, J. M. (1999). The seven principles for making marriage work. Crown Publishers.

Gottman, J. M., & Levenson, R. W. (2000). The timing of divorce: Predicting when a couple will divorce over a 14-year period. Journal of Marriage and Family, 62(3), 737–745.

Gottman, J. M., & Levenson, R. W. (2000). The timing of divorce: Predicting when a couple will divorce over a 14-year period. Journal of Marriage and Family, 62(3), 737–745. https://doi.org/10.1111/j.1741-3737.2000.00737.x

Gottman, J. M., & Silver, N. (1999). The seven principles for making marriage work. Harmony Books.

Gottman, J. M., & Silver, N. (2015). The Seven Principles for Making Marriage Work. Harmony.

Herman, J. L. (1997). Trauma and recovery: The aftermath of violence, from domestic abuse to political terror. Basic Books.

Herman, J. L. (2015). Trauma and recovery: The aftermath of violence, from domestic abuse to political terror (2nd ed.). Basic Books.

Holmes, B. M., & Rempel, J. K. (2012). Remembering our past: The role of memory in romantic relationships. Journal of Social and Personal Relationships, 29(3), 384–405.

Huston, T. L., & Melz, H. (2004). The case for (promoting) marriage: The devil is in the details. Journal of Marriage and Family, 66(4), 943–958.

Huston, T. L., & Melz, H. (2004). The case for (promoting) marriage: The devil is in the details. Journal of Marriage and Family, 66(4), 943–958. https://doi.org/10.1111/j.0022-2445.2004.00064.x

Janoff-Bulman, R. (1992). Shattered assumptions: Towards a new psychology of trauma. Free Press.

Johnson, S. M. (2008). Hold Me Tight: Seven Conversations for a Lifetime of Love. Little, Brown Spark.

Johnson, S. M. (2019). Attachment theory in practice: Emotionally focused therapy (EFT) with individuals, couples, and families. Guilford Publications.

Kashdan, T. B., Barrios, V., Forsyth, J. P., & Steger, M. F. (2014). Experiential avoidance as a generalized psychological vulnerability: Comparisons with coping and emotion regulation strategies. Behavior Research and Therapy, 44(9), 1301–1320.

Kelley, H. H., et al. (2013). An atlas of interpersonal situations. Cambridge University Press.

Keltner, D., & Bonanno, G. A. (1997). A study of laughter and dissociation: Distinct correlates of laughter and smiling during bereavement. Journal of Personality and Social Psychology, 73(4), 687–702.

Koole, S. L. (2009). The psychology of emotion regulation: An integrative review. Cognition and Emotion, 23(1), 4–41. https://doi.org/10.1080/02699930802619031

Lerner, H. G. (1985). The dance of anger: A woman's guide to changing the patterns of intimate relationships. HarperCollins.

Levine, A., & Heller, R. (2010). Attached: The new science of adult attachment and how it can help you find, and keep, love. TarcherPerigee.

Levine, P. A. (1997). Waking the tiger: Healing trauma. North Atlantic Books.

Levine, P. A. (2010). In an unspoken voice: How the body releases trauma and restores goodness. North Atlantic Books.

Linehan, M. M. (1993). Cognitive-behavioral treatment of borderline personality disorder. Guilford Press.

Linehan, M. M. (2014). DBT® skills training manual (2nd ed.). Guilford Press.

Linehan, M. M. (2014). DBT® skills training manual. Guilford Publications.

Lisak, D., & Miller, P. M. (2002). Repeat rape and multiple offending among undetected rapists. Violence and Victims, 17(1), 73–84.

Main, M., & Solomon, J. (1990). Procedures for identifying infants as disorganized/disoriented during the Ainsworth Strange Situation. In M. T. Greenberg, D. Cicchetti, & E. M. Cummings (Eds.), Attachment in the preschool years: Theory, research, and intervention (pp. 121–160). University of Chicago Press.

Markman, H. J., Rhoades, G. K., Stanley, S. M., Ragan, E. P., & Whitton, S. W. (2010). The premarital communication roots of marital distress and divorce: The first five years of marriage. Journal of Family Psychology, 24(3), 289–298.

McCrae, R. R., & Costa, P. T. (1999). A five-factor theory of personality. In L. A. Pervin & O. P. John (Eds.), Handbook of personality: Theory and research (2nd ed., pp. 139–153). Guilford Press.

Mikulincer, M., & Shaver, P. R. (2007). Attachment in adulthood: Structure, dynamics, and change. Guilford Press.

Mikulincer, M., & Shaver, P. R. (2016). Attachment in adulthood: Structure, dynamics, and change (2nd ed.). Guilford Press.

Najavits, L. M. (2002). Seeking safety: A treatment manual for PTSD and substance abuse. Guilford Press.

Neff, K. D. (2011). Self-compassion: The proven power of being kind to yourself. William Morrow.

Neff, L. A., & Karney, B. R. (2009). Acknowledging the elephant in the room: How stressful circumstances affect marriage. Current Directions in Psychological Science, 18(2), 126–130.

Neff, L. A., & Karney, B. R. (2009). Stress crossover in newlywed marriage: A longitudinal and dyadic perspective. Journal of Marriage and Family, 71(3), 546–559.

Neff, L. A., & Karney, B. R. (2009). Stress crossover in newlywed marriage: A longitudinal and dyadic perspective. Journal of Marriage and Family, 71(3), 594–607. https://doi.org/10.1111/j.1741-3737.2009.00622.x

Ogden, P., Minton, K., & Pain, C. (2006). Trauma and the body: A sensorimotor approach to psychotherapy. W. W. Norton & Company.

Orbuch, T. (2012). 5 simple steps to take your marriage from good to great. Delacorte Press.

Overall, N. C., & McNulty, J. K. (2017). What type of communication during conflict is beneficial for intimate relationships? Current Opinion in Psychology, 13, 1–5.

Overall, N. C., & McNulty, J. K. (2017). What type of communication during conflict is beneficial for intimate relationships? Current Opinion in Psychology, 13, 1–5. https://doi.org/10.1016/j.copsyc.2016.03.002

Panksepp, J. (1998). Affective neuroscience: The foundations of human and animal emotions. Oxford University Press.

Patterson, G. R. (2002). The early development of coercive family processes. In J. B. Reid, G. R. Patterson, & J. Snyder (Eds.), Antisocial behavior in children and adolescents: A developmental analysis and model for intervention (pp. 25–44). American Psychological Association.

Perel, E. (2017). The state of affairs: Rethinking infidelity. Harper.

Pietromonaco, P. R., & Powers, S. I. (2015). Attachment and health-related physiological stress processes. Current Opinion in Psychology, 1, 34–39. https://doi.org/10.1016/j.copsyc.2014.11.007

Pietromonaco, P. R., & Powers, S. I. (2015). Attachment and health-related physiological stress processes. Current Opinion in Psychology, 1, 34–39. https://doi.org/10.1016/j.copsyc.2014.11.015

Porges, S. W. (2011). The polyvagal theory: Neurophysiological foundations of emotions, attachment, communication, and self-regulation. W. W. Norton & Company.

Randall, A. K., & Bodenmann, G. (2017). Stress and its associations with relationship satisfaction. Current Opinion in Psychology, 13, 96–106. https://doi.org/10.1016/j.copsyc.2016.05.010

Rozin, P., & Royzman, E. B. (2001). Negativity bias, negativity dominance, and contagion. Personality and Social Psychology Review, 5(4), 296–320.

Sapolsky, R. M. (2004). Why zebras don't get ulcers. Holt Paperbacks.

Scheinkman, M., & Werneck, D. (2010). The multi-generational transmission of relational conflict: A dialogical and integrative approach. Family Process, 49(3), 303–318. https://doi.org/10.1111/j.1545-5300.2010.01327.x

Siegel, D. J. (2010). The mindful therapist: A clinician's guide to mindsight and neural integration. W. W. Norton & Company.

Siegel, D. J. (2012). The developing mind: How relationships and the brain interact to shape who we are (2nd ed.). Guilford Press.

Simpson, J. A., & Overall, N. C. (2013). Partner buffering of attachment insecurity. Current Directions in Psychological Science, 22(3), 234–239.

Solomon, A. (2017). *Loving bravely: Twenty lessons of self-discovery to help you get the love you want.* New Harbinger.

Stosny, S. (2013). *Living and loving after betrayal: How to heal from emotional abuse, deceit, infidelity, and chronic resentment.* New Harbinger Publications.

Tatkin, S. (2012). *Wired for Love: How Understanding Your Partner's Brain and Attachment Style Can Help You Defuse Conflict and Build a Secure Relationship.* New Harbinger Publications.

Tatkin, S. (2016). *Wired for love: How understanding your partner's brain and attachment style can help you defuse conflict and build a secure relationship.* New Harbinger.

Ting-Toomey, S. (2005). Identity negotiation theory: Crossing cultural boundaries. *Theorizing About Intercultural Communication,* 211–233.

Ting-Toomey, S., & Oetzel, J. G. (2001). *Managing intercultural conflict effectively.* Sage.

Van der Kolk, B. (2014). *The body keeps the score: Brain, mind, and body in the healing of trauma.* Viking.American Psychiatric Association. (2013). *Diagnostic and statistical manual of mental disorders* (5th ed.). Arlington, VA: American Psychiatric Publishing.

Walker, L. E. (2016). *The battered woman syndrome* (3rd ed.). Springer Publishing.

Wampler, K. S., & Shi, L. (2003). The Psychometric Properties of the Spouse Observation Checklist-Revised. *Journal* of Marital and Family Therapy, 29(1), 97–109. https://doi.org/10.1111/j.1752-0606.2003.tb00385.x

Widiger, T. A., & Trull, T. J. (2007). Plate tectonics in the classification of personality disorder: Shifting to a dimensional model. American Psychologist, 62(2), 71–83. https://doi.org/10.1037/0003-066X.62.2.71

Wile, D. B. (1993). After the honeymoon: How conflict can improve your relationship. Wiley.

Wood, J. T. (2013). Gendered lives: Communication, gender, and culture (10th ed.). Cengage Learning.

Zak, P. J. (2012). The physiology of moral sentiments. Journal of Economic Behavior & Organization, 77(1), 53–65.

Also by Renae C. Linde

Toxic No More: Proven Strategies to Overcome Destructive Patterns and Build Emotional Intelligence for Strong, Healthy Relationships

If *Fighting for Love* exposed your patterns, *Toxic No More* gives you the tools to change them. Through clear, actionable guidance and deep emotional insight, this book helps you set boundaries, defuse manipulative behaviors, and rebuild trust, from the inside out. Whether you're in the middle of a storm or rebuilding after one, this is your practical roadmap to healthier relationships.

When We Let Go: The Quiet Collapse of Effort, Ambition, and Responsibility

Where does personal accountability go when systems and relationships soften beyond recognition? This searing cultural critique weaves narrative with social analysis to expose the psychological roots of helplessness, the fatigue of caretakers, and the slow erosion of selfhood in modern life. Perfect for readers ready to confront the emotional cost of over-functioning and the weight of chronic dependency in families and society.

Available in Winter 2026.

Into the Void: Exploring the Mystery Between Death, Time, and Eternity

Grief dismantles time. What happens when connection ends, not in rupture, but in silence? This reflective, poetic inquiry wrestles with the imperceptible line between breath and eternity. For readers drawn to spiritual paradox, existential questions, and the emotional gravity of absence, this book offers not resolution, but reverent inquiry.

www.ingramcontent.com/pod-product-compliance
Lightning Source LLC
Chambersburg PA
CBHW020532030426
42337CB00013B/825